SUCCESSFUL TRAGEDIES

Priscila Uppal is a Canadian poet and fiction writer of South Asian descent. Born in Ottawa in 1974, she lives in Toronto. She has a PhD in English Literature and is a professor of Humanities and English at York University in Toronto. Her first UK poetry selection *Successful Tragedies: Poems 1998-2010* (Bloodaxe Books, 2010) draws on seven collections of poetry published in Canada: *How to Draw Blood from a Stone* (1998), *Confessions of a Fertility Expert* (1999), *Pretending to Die* (2001), *Live Coverage* (2003), *Holocaust Dream* (with photographs by Daniel Ehrenworth, 2005), *Ontological Necessities* (2006) and *Traumatology* (2010). *Ontological Necessities* was shortlisted for the prestigious $50,000 Griffin Prize for Excellence in Poetry.

Her other books include the novels *The Divine Economy of Salvation* (2002) and *To Whom It May Concern* (2009), and the critical study *We Are What We Mourn: The Contemporary English-Canadian Elegy* (2009). She also edited the multilingual *Exile Book of Poetry in Translation: 20 Canadian Poets Take On the World* (2009) and *The Exile Book of Canadian Sports Stories* (2009).

Priscila Uppal's website: www.priscilauppal.ca

PRISCILA UPPAL

Successful
Tragedies

POEMS 1998-2010

BLOODAXE BOOKS

ISBN: 978 1 85224 860 4

First published 2010 by
Bloodaxe Books Ltd,
Highgreen,
Tarset,
Northumberland NE48 1RP.

www.bloodaxebooks.com
For further information about Bloodaxe titles
please visit our website or write to
the above address for a catalogue.

Supported by
**ARTS COUNCIL
ENGLAND**

Cover design: Neil Astley & Pamela Robertson-Pearce.

Printed in Great Britain by
Bell & Bain Limited, Glasgow, Scotland.

For Christopher
& our surviving through every success
& every tragedy

ACKNOWLEDGEMENTS

This book is selected from *How to Draw Blood from a Stone* (Exile Editions, 1998), *Confessions of a Fertility Expert* (Exile Editions, 1999), *Pretending to Die* (Exile Editions, 2001), *Holocaust Dream* (MacLaren Art Centre, 2003), *Live Coverage* (Exile Editions, 2003), *Poem for a Runaway Mother* in *Red Silk: An Anthology of South-Asian Canadian Women Poets* (Mansfield Press, 2004), *Ontological Necessities* (Exile Editions, 2006) and *Traumatology* (Exile Editions, 2010). Many thanks to my loyal Canadian publishing house, Exile Editions, as well as to all the editors, publishers, translators, grant and prize judges, festival and reading series organisers, family, friends, York University, and others who have championed my work in my homeland and abroad.

Thanks to Helen Walsh at Diaspora Dialogues, London Literature Festival, the Canadian High Commission, and Graham Henderson from Poet in the City for bringing my work to the attention of UK publishers and audiences.

Many, many thanks to Neil Astley and Bloodaxe Books for making a dream come true.

And my love and endless thanks to Christopher Doda, who can't wait to mark his calendar.

CONTENTS

I may die before my time.
I may live *before my time.*

GILLIAN ROSE

from

HOW TO DRAW BLOOD
FROM A STONE

(1998)

How to Draw Blood from a Stone

On family afternoons
the digging begins.
It begins with your hands.

You carry the stones like stillborn babies,
lay them down.
So closely the heads rise
from brown wet beds.

You add others when it rains,
when you're sad.
You name them all
by holding them down.

In winter they sit patiently
amongst the cold.
You stare wondering
what they want,
so close to the earth
and still.

This is not a place you go to speak.
The stones bleed through
the soil.

This is not a graveyard.
You can't apologise.

Bone-marrow

Trees know each other by their bark.
Everything alive has developed a language.
Even thunder, even death.

Children are obsessed with mirrors
trying to pry the glass free
to release the twin who understands their every move
and face.

Lovers despair the moment
they no longer find a reflection
in each other's tears.

Look at science:
Desperately in love with itself searching
for solar systems identical to ours.
Signs of life.

For want of bone-marrow
the entire kingdom was lost.

Think about why religions fail.

Ghosts

All the lies you were told
about the ways of ghosts.
They don't come out at night.
Nor do they scream or cry
or crave your body.

No doors knock or windows rattle.
Nothing moves.
They are always there.
The secret of ghosts
is how they disappear,
start a new life –
get out of the house.

You keep the kitchen spotless.
Fresh flowers on the window sill,
porch lamps lit, and hands flat
as the table where you sit
praying for the phone to ring.

You don't dare sleep in case
you miss him. Waiting the way
you did during the war:
for a white light – a hand – someone
you could follow away.

When god created

A latch-key kid from the beginning
he was a lonely child
the kind who needs imaginary friends
just to get by,
afraid of the dark.

Left alone for a week
he pushed the floor from the ceiling
drew plants and fruit on the walls
when he got hungry
counted the days and nights
through his window.

He saw winged creatures
and sea-monsters on his blankets
beasts and cattle on hardwood tables
filled the air with other children
and multiplied
multiplied
with every worried breath.

He heard his heart out loud.
He saw that it was good and
rested while creatures sniffed
the earth and fought.

On the eighth day he rubbed his eyes
forgot the universe made up in a corner
of his bedroom
and played only with stars.

The Politics of Fire

My mother burned our house
down when I was twelve. Only
the trees bent back to see
the walls crumble.

I let my children play
with matches, to understand
the discipline it takes to
cover before striking.

Palms

The Fool cups the world
in his hands, arms raised with eyes
up, a foot sliding over a cliff.

My mother inherited foresight
from her mother.
She has learned to deal
with one hand, and the kitchen
revolves over her fingers like
the flame of the candle beside her.

She knows about lines
on hands and fists.
Which lines to cross
and which to not.

Clothes packed and unpacked
shuffled and misplaced, her family
heirlooms hidden in her sleeves.

She tells me time is no fool.
The world is not a wound-up clock
forgotten and waiting to stop.

Lines predict weather,
a storm or drizzle of visitors
in patterns, and here, in a kitchen
with her agile fingers, I believe her.

The door opens and slams.
The candle blows out.
Dinner is late.

In the morning her face
spread by fingerprints.
My grip on her body, her palm on the burner,
erasing the life she doesn't want,
me clinging to her sliding feet.

The Retired Orchestra

Once a year at night the home on Queen Street
becomes a symphony. My grandfather,
probably an oboe, should be in this home.
He never passed up a dance with a lady
or the chance to sing a round.

They steal away from numbered rooms
and meet in the cafeteria. All the instruments tuned up
scaling their throats and shaking off
dust from their strings.

Large-bellied basses set the tone. Trombones clear
away tables, call in the flutes and the violins,
women with pursed lips who finger the air and sway.
Turned trays are drums, soup cans from the trash
become a xylophone, newcomers play the spoons
and conductors stand keeping the beat with sugar drips
sucked like long flat reeds.

Legs kick between sets – some whistle
and hoot, throw up their hands or pills, grab the arm
of the one beside them, unplug the clock,
spill salt shakers until the curtain of dawn
arises.

In the morning nurses and orderlies will wake
struggling with a hum from their dreams
as the orchestra retires to bed for another year
the fierce and strong notes that have held on
for a lifetime.

Fatherless angels

They are almost all fatherless these days,
unless they have many,
their eyes fallen like seeds from sunflowers
or daffodils, yellow and
drifting

I've seen them with their wings stretched wide
jumping in front of cars
with signs on their backs and luggage stuffed
between feathers.
They don't care where they go,
they just want to go somewhere else.

All the street maps to heaven are sold
wrapped in plastic
directions to movie stars and palm trees
hot in their hands, sweaty and flat
like lottery tickets.

I was stabbed by an angel once,
right in my side
when I wasn't looking.
Neither was he.
Sorry, he said, I thought
you were my dad.

Fellatio

I'm sculpting a tiny death
in my potter's wheel
your skin ripples in motion
in time with the hum

Water is used to soften
the unformed clay
my lips knead and
mould a living wave

An exercise in timing
to link hand with heat
once in the kiln
every flaw will show

A suicide art moving
with a cry into me
and I'm left with tears
of a crouching child.

I wonder why I worked
so hard just to empty you
to have what I shaped
slip down from my hands

Warning to a Gynaecologist

Remember that you have seen further than many:

Tested the waters;
Canals, escape routes, and waterfalls,
Visions of the red sea.

From an open sea-shell you've heard
An ocean in waiting.

Chart the territory with a prophet's diligence.

Be careful what you take:

You could push away kin almost forgotten
Or dislodge an angel I buried in the field.

An Apology for Dying Young

I was made
of sheet lightning
which is why my life
was shockingly short.

If you look closely
you can still see my coded
poems in the sky,
unsigned.

How Stars Make Love

Not so quickly as one might think.
In the sky everything takes time –
there's so much space to travel.

They're afraid we might be watching
through a telescope or one of those probes,
so they wait perfectly still
shining in their loneliness.

Wearing dresses of sequins,
stars ache for daylight
wave their lashes through the milky way
pout with lips of burnt candy.

Millions of years between them before
they touch, stars are shy of contact
creep back to safe places
parts of town they know best
until they're almost too old to care.

It's the last light that streaks the sky
when stars make love
right before they die

hey you, fella, hang on to me
please hold me tight,
I'm just about to fall –

careful careful

if you drop this poem
it won't forgive you
won't return even one
of your calls it will
pass you by on the street
looking the other way
with shades on and heeled
shoes and never will it
trust you again or lie
in your arms or care if
you cry or even stop to
watch you fall it has no
time for you if you can't
hold for just a second
wait for it to adjust
to the bumps in your hands
remember if you drop this
poem with certainty
it will never admit it
ever loved you, not to anyone

When god died

Sure, the madmen predicted it,
But no one took them seriously.

The priests had no idea.
Just another body to deliver,
Some people to comfort.

It made the local news:
A child who needed a transplant.

And some opened their purses,
Emptied out what was left at the end
Of the month.

A few joined the family,
Left flowers at the graveyard.
Thinking they hadn't really
known him, god willing,
They might have.

The new heart, unfortunately, was rejected.
The madmen wept uncontrollably.

People said the usual things:
He could've been something
Could've had the world at his feet
That kid didn't even get a chance.

Theory

When the earth was flat
you were wary of travel.

Now your fear is circular.

That you will find nowhere
but home.

The Third Fate

When the time comes you will
be led to your bed.

The midwife will arrive and
a bell to ring for water.

Skin will sink stitched
into eyes and bone.

Two sisters will abandon you.
You will have no father.

All loose threads will be tied.

She will take your knitted life
and lay it on top of you.

You will begin to see symmetry
in the dark.

A mother's voice will say:

You have lived long enough
in this form.

Here is your cocoon:
Become a butterfly.

from

CONFESSIONS OF
A FERTILITY EXPERT

(1999)

My Heart

It is a lullaby I remember hearing
       from the nest of a crib.

It is a lie I told once
       to keep strangers at bay.

It is outside my grasp
       like a feather falling in the afternoon.

It is responsible for my blood
       and I can't blame it for anything.

       It is red.

It is a brief note I meant to write
       to you.

It is a canary that doesn't want loose
       from his cage.

It is a hunter, stalking, with footsteps
       timed as horses' hooves.

       It is red.

It is a wound from a battle
       I don't quite remember.

It is not an enemy or a friend.

It is an eloquent negotiator, and I
try to keep my head straight,
       away from its eyes
begging me to let it eat itself out.

My Birth

Blind, I carved myself
in the darkness:
teeth from teeth
hair from hair
blood from blood
my soul from her heavy water.

I remember a fall
purple as plums in spring
and a parting of waves
screams that still rise in dreams
like the echo of sinking ships.

I must have said 'Let there be light'
for there it appeared
stronger than any love
costlier than any freedom since.

From then on
there would be a wall between us
thick as sky

pushing me away from
the promised land
that all the colours of a rainbow
can't ever make up for.

Childhood Study: Sally

Other girls at first said yes
took the fifty cents and licorice whips
then folded into tears when they understood
what game I wanted to play.
They were children.

Sally did it for free.
Broken in by her father
the tender age of seven
ever since threw up her skirt
and claimed she was a woman
among the little boys.

Behind the back of my house
she stripped off her dress like old
wallpaper, spread her legs in a perfect V
and was beautiful on the yellow grass
as I entered her.

She was the reason for being alive
and the reason for being alive.

I wept like a flower in the morning
my first dew emerging alive
from the sweet equator of her thighs.

Fairy Godmothers

From the beginning I believed
God was a woman
who brought milk and cheese
and clothes as well as bread
whose kingdom was reigned
by stroking hands and warm blankets.

In gardens I grabbed flowers
made daisy-chains and dandelion hearts
felt the wind behind my ears
singing softly:
scatter, young man, scatter.

I prayed to her
pushing inside with my legs
back raised like the roof
of a peasant cathedral.

The girls I took there turned
green and restless in the sun
burned by fire
and dancing on tiptoes
their dresses billowing upwards
like wafting clouds.

And where I looked
trees swayed
branches spoke time
and fairy godmothers warned us all
that 'Magic cannot last past midnight.
Take your mate and trespass the earth.'

Ovarian Dreams

Inside you the gaseous spiral swirls
a night parade of stars and meteors
plant fires for the BigBang.
Solar system, red.

The seeds of children pass through fields
hunting and begging for water.
You let down your bridge.
Fetal, fortress.

Underwater, bed.
A waterfall of tears.
You open and close
release a pearl.

You came and came and came.
You are still coming,
orgasms like ripples of an earthquake.

I remember the first night I dreamt of stealing
back between your thighs
I wrapped my arms around your neck
like a stethoscope
and listened to your heart for hours.

Fertility Issue

When you first arrive I detect the signs:

an uneasy shift in your legs and eyes
the serious study of documents on the walls
an inevitable look of desperate belief.

You want a baby,
believe I can warp life into your image,
believe the universe is a carefully constructed
white lie.

What you don't understand and what I don't offer
is this:

You want a baby,
and I do not draw out life
or witness it
like a good-natured incarnate god.
I am more of a philosopher,
assessing whether or not it exists.

Fertilisation Study

1st Month

soilbed horizon
ghostflower you haunt
stamen and pistil
hush of genesis

2nd Month

airbred seedlings
umbrella sky
an eye heavy lidded
with pollen

3rd Month

rootclinger
you weave darkness
force black earth
to mold you

4th Month

germination cloud
you suck softly
shoots of dew
geranium

5th Month

rosebud fingers
arrangement of blood
sense a faint beat
blooming

6th Month

young miner
taps ore
sand stones
crafts a sturdy stem

7th Month

petal pairs
vineyard synthesis
vessel a vase
centerpiece

8th Month

lilypad blanket
you float mimelike
tears across her belly
waterraft

9th Month

come spring
laying laurels
blessed bestowing
of fruit

Ultrasounds

His sex pronounced upon the film
a small boy struck bells.
Hand across ribcage bellowed
a deep-throated wave of a cello.
I was surrounded in symphony.

My ears trained by day in light
tuned
grabbed at the notes
of castaways.
The darkness seemed to feed me
like a placenta.

Countless negatives
netted me in their seascape.
Along the cold steel tables
atoms trembled.
Twin girls with tadpole tails
blew kisses and called me sailor.
Until then I had never heard the ocean speak.

I cocked shells and waded in sand.
The air grew arteries around me
while boys and girls barely breathing
surpassed the alumni of heavenly choirs.

The Egg

Twenty years ago an egg
was found by my heel.

It waits like a good soldier
for a fight I haven't declared
a disease I haven't yet isolated.

In it could be millions of fossils,
creatures never seen or named,
tight and ready to burst like the seed
of a select pomegranate
or a system of grief so complex that one look
could brand you blind.

Wherever I tread, the egg watches,
my heel aches with the sword
of an unknown slayer
come for its white curves.

If I can heal
it will be through the image of an egg
and what it could possibly contain.

What I Learned in Physics

where matter aches most
        is at its core
       I am simply
the fingerprint of an atom

Beauty Contest

I have touched secret places
wells of health you spring from.
Inside your body are rotations
fascinating as a solar system.

Your cells cities.
Your glands planets.
Your atoms compressed like bombs.
And blood constantly creating you.

If I held a beauty contest
five senses would be necessary
and judges with x-ray vision.

And you would be my reigning queen:
perfect arteries
a seductive spleen
impenetrable bones
and a heart as warm and salty as the ocean floor.

The Lady or the Tiger

You lay down to sleep
after another attempt
and in the twilight I can almost trace
the path my love has taken.

(my tiny warriors hot with rage – I see them
hungry, weary,
sluggish
                        maps of you
in glossy books – ovaries opening
and closing like hidden rooms)

On your backside I see charmed faces
and grateful handshakes
when I of all people who have studied the odds
know they are stacked for losing.

For the next forty-eight hours
millions of children will drown
while maybe, maybe one will tear you down

and I've become an insomniac, jealous of your sleep
exhausted by endless defeat.

Rome Wasn't Built in a Day

From the egg I plan to build a city
glistening and elegant
with gold archways and trees the size
of tall buildings

the sky will change colour
and only those who fly will enter
its fiery gates

I have peered inside the egg
(though the shell is hard)
the way a gypsy's crystal calls up
the future

the city has not begun to rise
it is waiting
staying egg for now

the sky will change colour
and only those who die will enter
its fiery gates

Rome wasn't built in a day.
Eden was.

Letter to the Child I Will Never Have

Dear   ,

When you called I listened
my ear to the ground,
divining you,
            praying for water.

I read up on bones
bodies preserved in mud
supposing you trapped
            studied survival.

I walked days and nights
in deserts. Burned bushes.
Sold my soul for a shovel
        and began to dig.

A trickster earth
spelled out your name
drilled eyes shifted
            rock into a spine.

Fondly I excavated.
Walls collapsed.
Legs stuck in quicksand.
            Life lines dissolved.

Every second erosion
fills your grave. I want
you to know seasons
            are not circular.

And whatever rumours
may find you, know no
matter what people say
            you were wanted.

After-life

For those who are hungry
      food is placed just beyond reach
For those who are tired
      sleep descends then breaks like a mirage
For those who are lonely
      loved ones pry mutely outside the door
For those who are guilty
      water lends no release of thirst
For those who are sickly
      bones crack and crumble inside you
For those who are healthy
      a constant chill is your companion
For those who are weary
      staircases keep spiraling upward
For those who are skeptics
      pain becomes real
For those who are here
      patience is needed
For those of you where we were
      Cry   Cry   to be born

from

PRETENDING TO DIE

(2001)

Searching the Dictionary

After your death I took to reading.
Not the classics you had in mind we would enjoy
together; *Othello*, *A Tale of Two Cities*, *Madame Bovary*
or *War and Peace*. It wasn't narrative I sought (what did I care
about the intrigues of kings or bored French wives), or even poetry
(no one could convince me of beauty, prosody, terrible
transcendence). I wanted the one word that would speak you.
I ransacked the dictionary.

Nothing came close. Adjectives and adverbs were all
distraught. Words like *here*, or *there*,
quietly, *gently*, *goodnight*. Haunting me in the strangest
places, between leaves on the ground by our walkway
or the grocery line-up where hands grabbed food
demanding *cans*, *cartons*, *bottles*, *boxes*. But where
were you hiding?

So I delved into words that crossed between places: *merge*,
blend, *saturate*, *osmosis*. Words that broke: *crack*, *wedge*,
distill, *violate*. Words that stung: *missing*, *vacant*, *error*, *love*.
All were inadequate, as is the word *inadequate*: insufficient, not
capable or competent, lacking.

And I refuse to go to the Old Book, the First Dictionary.
Christ never impressed me. He was all love. He got
to come back and say *so long* properly, *see you later*
and know it would be true.
            There is no word to describe the way
I touch you and can't touch you simply sitting on a streetcar
or sipping my soup, nor the sense of disintegration
I feel every time the phone rings. No
word for how I've started to divide my friends
in terms of those I can afford to lose and those I can't.

Pretending To Die

When I dug myself into the muddy sand
the waves seemed to roll
with new vigour. The sun burnt delirious
eyelids, I desperately tried but couldn't
keep closed.

Perchance there would be screams
and sirens, a frantic mob shedding tears,
a new mother to cradle my limp
flesh and strap her lips
firmly on mine.

Instead the tide washed in
bearing seaweed and popsicle sticks
a little girl stole my pail
even the sand abandoned me
while the one I loved for three full summers
stepped squarely upon my ribs
and kept on going.

Purgatory

I will meet you in purgatory with the other
outcasts, bare-faced and oblivious.
I will meet you in the elevator
stuck on the eleventh floor with a bouquet
of white roses and a silver pocket watch.

There we will discuss the effects of claustrophobia.
We will try on each other's shoes.
We will place our fingers in wire sockets
and scream like the dead.

But we will not be dead. In limbo the words
we dread to utter suspend like flashing numbers.
We will invade the space. Make ourselves room.

Come to answer for the times we sort-of sinned,
kind-of helped, perhaps guessed the right answer.

You will argue you had little to work with. Show them
stained hands. I will assert my soul was switched

at birth. The light will guide us. Eyes closed, knees broken – we will
continue to rise. Betray our disguise.
The fires, my friend, will not touch you.

Turning to Salt

It begins with a peel of wallpaper
a camera's sharp lens
and soon a curtain of eyes
replaces your clothes.

It begins with the simplest desire:
ceiling plaster melts and carpets
rip. Ants are having a field day.
Broken mirrors the least
of the year's disasters.

When my touch begins to burn
like my father's did (*one arm
asleep – the pins and needles – the other
doesn't seem to belong to me. Stand
back.*) pack the bags.

Promise me, if I am crumbling
don't look. Feel free
to grab your wife (keep clear
of dust) and storm out
of the collapsing city.

Lament

In the interim (while I still have a voice), I must
open my mouth like a large cave and find animals
dwelling inside building shelters, foraging for food,
carving up rock into myth and resurrected rituals.

Regardless of progress, the winds still turn bitter
in November and illness comes like a thief, subtle
and wicked. The holes in my eyes have no place
to hide and the coming slaughter is a surety.

So I can do nothing but notice this crippled flower,
this twisted leg on a yellow bird. Bless the child
holding out her tired hand for change. Acknowledge
the old man throwing stones against church stairs

and wait my turn. There are laments for the lost, the weary,
the dead. Laments for those who speak for their people
and those who have no people to speak for. For the land.
For the seasons passing. For gravediggers and water diviners.

Everyone we meet, we know is temporary. So why, why,
do tribal memories insist on clinging to our skins?
Inside the wilderness of my mouth, a lion roars for the first
time today. Knows this pain he is born with is certainly ours.

Imagining a Bullet

Before the invention of guns
It was possible to kill
By shutting one eye
And aiming for the heart.

The Modern Soul

Flat and shiny as the silver dollar
I keep hidden in my bedroom drawer.
Its value may decrease year by year
But I'd still bet my entire future
That some day, one dark stranger
Will fight me to the death for it.

Foretelling God

In the beginning, before this world was created, God was created by a young man on his way to the hospital. He had an itch in his throat that couldn't be reached and a pain in his side doubled him over. Still, he insisted on walking to Emergency so he could stop in the park, smell the flowers and wave to his favourite counter girl at the coffee shop. There his dog lay waiting, paws tucked tenderly under his chin.

At the door he fainted and the nurses all screamed. Declared, 'He must go to surgery, right away.' 'What will they do?' he cried. 'Cut out the place that hurts,' they replied. 'Won't I miss it?' 'No, it is nothing. Nothing.' 'Then don't bother to save it for me,' the young man vowed. 'Shove the stone in a jar and call it God.' 'Count to seven,' the anesthetist told him, 'and it will soon be over.'

My Ambition

I wanted to know
what it was like to be my father
so I left my country with nothing but a letter
and a scholarship that was revoked
as soon as I landed. Went to work
for an Englishman
who sold books he couldn't read.
At night paid the day's wages
for language lessons from another immigrant.

Next I took a job and worked
my way up to manager, and knew
I was doing good, found a delicate wife,
a house with a reasonable mortgage,
a pool, a couple of kids,
and the kind of attitude my family
back home would not stand for.
I had arrived.

Then I shattered my spine with a stick
spent my life tied to a chair
begging for food and water
for my wife not to leave me
for my children's love on holidays.
I could barely afford to get my glasses fixed
to see the damage
let alone send my children to college.

Now I can sympathise
with the many letters
he writes to no one in particular
and the detailed ledgers he keeps in the basement
of canned goods and the number of foreign
news correspondents on television. It's important
to keep accounts
be able to predict what you can.

Yet when he calls me in the middle of the night
with another fact or statistic,
I hang up.

I have not fled from my hatred
but despise him more
seeing through his eyes
turning my ambition
into a suspicious game of chance
and pushing my withheld love
into the arms
of strangers.

If Abraham

If Abraham hadn't responded to God's command
how much better the relationship with his son
might have been. No nights of discomfort
in the dark, calling out in his sleep
for good Samaritans, no more fights
at breakfast about the day
it almost happened, no more hiding
the largest and sharpest kitchen knives.

If Abraham hadn't heard another word
and done the deed, how many days before some troupe
of angered parents hunted him down, stood
on his lawn with signs and government officials
broke every unbarred window
in his home, how many years before
the smell came off his hands,
before he could eat meat again.

If Abraham was smart as the men in my neighbourhood
he would have destroyed evidence of his plans,
taken the boy no further than the basement,
and kept the fires burning until
not a soul could have recognised that body.

Signs of Life

The Russian lady on the corner has begun
to keep the porch light on for her son,
who moved twenty years ago.

A street party burst spontaneously after the hockey game
and the loudest participants were cheering the losing team.

Two days ago the rosebush bloomed in spite of itself.

(I tell you this because there is a way out, out the back
of the kitchen if you jump over the drunk in the doorway
who's harmless anyway and find the extra key your ex left
under the mat hoping one day you'd follow. If you can still lift
your head and not gawk at the tower in the distance
but at the vision overhead, keep on til you feel water at
your feet; then there is time.)

An old man sells his Bible for a bag of candy.

The wheelchair, in the corner, collects dust.

My friends have filed for a mass divorce
from the past.

The spot on my clothing is not going to come out.

Stop: I tell you this because
a little girl on recess at the schoolyard
is scratching her name into the pavement until it bleeds.

In Your Sickness

It is your body, soft as an old bed,
the fleshy pillows of your fever
that make me want to deliver you like an old letter
back to a first love, aged yet tough, sitting
stout like a sandcastle on the beaches
of your lost land, waves curling and unfolding
like tides through your drowning speech.
She has perhaps forgotten you these
many years, her heart broken by stronger, crueler
men than you, her eyes the dried tunnels of travel
cursing the waters, the deep waters that bear men away.
I will say to her: here is the man I love,
you too once loved, fading now like a memory.
He is light and haze. He is specks of dust.
He has turned into a terrible mystery.
I want to bring you to her, tied in white sheets,
a welcoming ceremony in the ritualistic days
of sacrifice, days of parting. I want to hold
you in my arms the way we held our animals.
I want to flatten all your hair with my hand,
have you lick the lingering salt off my palm.

Afternoon Window Washer

While he naps I slip off the sheets
dip my gloves into the pail
and start to work.

I strip off his clothes and dump them
in the hamper.

Scrub his skin until it's white
clean of birthmarks
and freckles, erased of moles.
Hair falls like dead grass
collected in my hands.

If he wakes he knows to keep silent
and still. I have a job to do
and will not stop until everything is
spotless.

Pupils recede and his chest
becomes hard as an ironing board.

Then with bare fingernails I get
at the dirt in tough places: the bellybutton
and armpits. Between eyelashes.
I file his toes, until he is

perfectly clear and I can
see straight through him into
his neighbour's backyard.

Sex with Columbus

We rode the waves in a month-long stretch
of glorious discovery. My body meeting him
like a welcome error: odd instrument of his
marking round territory.

It was supposed to be a secret between us
and the sea.

Later I heard he bragged to his buddies.
Claimed to be the first, though he wasn't.

Five Short Poems for Your Amusement at the Hospital

I

Manage your room like a hotel.
Phone down for food
and flowers. Be conspicuous
about guests.

Steal the robes.

II

Think of the things you've chased:
your brother when he was small
and used to pinch your cheeks, the moon,
the cat next door in the garden,
streetlights when they turn too fast, the rain,
fire, bureaucrats, all kinds of balls, lovers,
the express bus, shame, your mother's
memory.

Think that the world must now
come to you.

III

The kidneys are outrageous organs
greedy and unkind
they unwind
by punching people
in the ribs.

Who wants to make peace
with them anyway?

IV

The nurse and doctor have been
having an affair
for the last month

hot for each other
they run their hands on your belly
burning up

and you are the embers
keeping romance alive.

V

When they insist on taking more blood
and x-rays
pretend you are a prehistoric mammal
they are laying bare
to read your bones
uncover how you managed to survive
all this time.

Hairless

She's been told
it's a disease

runs her fingers through
the hair
like an untamed cat

grips loose
strands in her fist
like a jaw

she can't stand the mess
the uncleanliness
of the dead

strips them bare
sends them down the stream
of her washtub

one for her father, that man
she called hunger
until he remarried

another torn
for her lover, she wore
like an old sweater
until not a thread remained

and an entire clump, gone
for the sister she never had
who would've
told her the secrets she'd
been left out of

five for the florist
who stalked her
an entire autumn

three for the trees
outside that lost
their leaves

as he stood, waiting*

four for the passenger who was never found
two for the letter that went missing
ten for the cat crushed in an engine
eight for the sky's fierce hand
one for the road

* There are nights the hairs return, those stubborn children of her brain, when
she has dreams of hands and feet and fists and clubs and flowers crushed in
medicine jars, stones pounded into eyes, fire exits, baby strollers, small men
in dark costumes and women wandering through the corridors she knows she
locked before going to bed.

The Lamp

My grandmother asked for our hands
and more lamplight before she died.
We told her the pain in her joints
was just the rain, bones shifting like clouds.
She would rise in the morning and I would curl
her limp and still black hair.

Mother brought water and vegetable soup.
We spoke about cucumbers
and smashed pale tomatoes
reminding ourselves that seasons
and grandmother's coughs are routine as spooning food.

She took it with grace and silence, her eyes
on the antique silver while I polished her mouth.
She took it with a promise we would follow
her wishes to the letter: one for the house, a second
for her soul, and the third she never could say.

Her eyes fixed on the lampshade's insolence
she dropped her lip
to draw a last breath
the last breath meant for a word.

She had three wishes, Genie, and you were not one of them.

Endings

After the funeral: time to say goodbye.
Keep up appearances, hold on to flowers
and make up speeches for ritual's sake.
But ritually there is no solace for suffering.

What we leave are not wilted petals, the pictures
of doves and pillars, fresh water at the entrance.
Nor the gentle handshakes, carefully labeled plates,
or thousands of white crumpled handkerchiefs.

Sense the room: the sounds are those of anticipation.
An audience silently awaits a new reception.
If sorrow were a door it would open from the inside.
If sorrow were a match it would strike when wet.

A time of stop, over, solitary ground.
For us, like in dreams, promise me two endings.

Because a Body Drowns not by an Excess of Water, But by a Lack of Air

all his grief is in his feet
in the stairwell where you used to hide and paint pictures
   of autumn trees and broken dreams
in the yard where the cicadas stretch their weary stems and swings
   sway in the push of the wind
in the shopping malls where you lined up kid by kid to make sure
   none were lost
he paces alongside store windows and display cases
   stares each mannequin in the eye

in the hospital corridors where you had your tonsils out decades ago
   and the nurses brought you cigarettes
in the train station where you took a last trip east
   claiming lost luggage and old neglected hats
in the four corners of the split highway where you could have gone to visit
   sister or mother, friend or brother
is a single sign that tells him there are five miles to go

he runs through fields of strawberries you crushed in your hand
   he runs past the bushels of blood

in the long corridors of the community centre
   between rummage sales and the gymnasium
in the parking lots
   beside florists and fruit stands
in the crammed blocks
   of the neighbourhood
in the double plots
   of the cemetery

it might be you he feels in the soles of his feet
   a slight bump, an ache
he can't locate
   a tick
he can't quite control

it might be you underneath the street in front of the house
you've never seen
making him trip

and it's the sewers he fears have taken you
moving from grate
          to grate
just out of earshot

          the water forced on
filled with dirt and rain and garbage and grief
he fears you'll drown
he fears you'll never come up again for air

A Second Chance

In autumn, the season of lepers, we turn our heads
for fear of catching the fever. The weary limbs of weather's travels
fall. The wind says, *I did not mean to cause such harm,*
it was the rain that forced my hand. And the rain repents,
those poor pretty flowers were such darlings.
I should not have drowned them.

In the wake of this new morning, the littered leaves and broken bulbs
are swept, water drains back to the river's mouth. The fine regret
of nights of misplaced passion, cold aggression, appear along the orchard
path. Groggy heads and aching temples bend the body down.
Is it true what happened? I must have succumbed to another voice.
I must have blacked out.

Somewhere, deep in the core of earth, a single believer signs
the season's petition. Winter's snow offers a clean white slate promise
of a second chance. And we make clear marks of our intentions
with sheltered feet, forgetful for a moment of summer's bones
struggling to stab the calm surface:
All right, prove to me this time you mean business.

The Car Thief

I begin with the trunk, prop
its lid open. Find
out if you're the type
to keep a spare tire, a booster cable,
bottles of antifreeze

or the kind who requires a mess
to keep moving
old candy wrappers, dirty sneakers,
lipstick tubes
and newspapers

ascertain whether
you are married or single by the small
items in your glove box
if you are childless
by the state of the mats.

I pull the steering wheel
to my lips,
feel if the seats are warm.

No question, it's an addiction.
I'm positive I could have fallen
for the woman who kept a map
of Italy on her dashboard.

No question.

I Refuse the Gift of Reincarnation

I don't want to begin again. Life, though
not half as glorious as once imagined
has at least come to order. Yes, I have
troubles: a drunk father, runaway mother,
a brother who insists I'm a fly on his wall,
and you may be able to fix that next time
around. And yes, my true Love disappeared
with all the money; but I've got a pre-nup
now and eat out three times a week.
There are worse disasters than these.

In my next life I might be raped, murdered,
sliced and diced and buried around this awful
city, or my skin might be the wrong colour
for the next regime. Or I might come
back a man and I'd laugh at myself all day –
probably not the path to enlightenment.

Imagine life as a butterfly, you tease. Please.
There is a score of them circling my house.
If the day is clear we collect them in jars.
If not, we watch them slam into glass.
There is not one of us now who isn't beautiful.

from

HOLOCAUST DREAM

(2003)

Barbed Wire Lens

∞

Barbed Wire Lens

The past is blurred, but our grief is not,
anxious like a baby bottle nib against
the inner wrist, the kind of late-night
haze where panic is an oversight,
longing a pant leg that gets stepped on.

So we take our dampness out, hang it
on trees as birdfeeders, as metal pails filled
with rain. The fence is tough and carved:
we can see the outline of your goodbyes,
the pantries guarded with poisoned locks.

We wear red to be recognised, reconciled
to the future, an anesthetic army of feet.
Remove the barbed wire from our hearts.
Discuss the cobblestones. Swear upon
breadcrumb trails. The answer cowers lost

in the woods, wishing for the grandmothers
to bring us home. Stuck with visiting hours
and prepared meals, the recorded messages
we try to derail. What if we are dry
as your eyes? Insipient as the weather?

What if I am stepping on your toes?
Can you forgive us? Can we readjust?
Can you ever be ours when you have never been let out?

∞

The Trees of Auschwitz

The bark endless, lingers like the lines of insolent wedding bells
secretly kept vows while temples and gods and skies are broken.

∞

The Extent of Anger

Who will bring you home? And if you agree,
how can I offer you a seat when the cushions are sewed
with my mother's tears, the officer's hate,
the entire town's terrible memories? Still

you say, sit, sit, stay and eat. We are all family. Look,
there is nothing but bread in the oven. And when I light a match
to the stove, the alarm sounds, the neighbours call the police.

Knives and spoons sit side by side, no one separates them.

∞

Proofs

Entire villages rise and fall in the darkroom.
In the darkroom entire villages fall and rise.

∞

Philosophy Is Not an Elixir

The road to the entertainment district was taken by buses two and nine.
There are celebrities on these marquees. Singers and trumpeters,
tap dancers, and acrobats. An entire orchestra practising.
Excuse me for this

intrusion. I want to pray
my respects. Over here,
I want to pray

something awful. Without you who will teach us the way
to the theatre? Who will discuss the merits of our attempt
at greatness and freedom in the arid corners

of cafés on the march? Your
eyes like tickets. Your wisdom
gates that open and shut.

from
LIVE COVERAGE
(2003)

Someone Ought to Set up a Shelter

for all the Greek ladies raped in the first two hundred pages alone
of Ovid's *Metamorphoses*, not that I'm in favour of censorship
or rewriting history to ease disturbed sleep
but I have a feeling these events really did transpire as told
and I'm supposed to know and *do* something

Isn't that why the dead come back – to force us to act? If not, should
I be fascinated by the legion of illegitimate children Jove fostered
unaware they were his? Am I requisitioned to recover
a lost will or secret stash? Open a charity or draft
a petition in the names of these children

comfort their mothers from this land: there is no rape here sweet Proserpina,
you will not be ravaged. I can't exactly lie to the dead. That would be worse
than doing nothing, don't you think? But what have we got here: shelters;
and since I'm no inventor I suppose I could build one between pages 76
and 77 and all the nymphs could hide-out there, escorted by Diana

but only after being raped
after they are no longer virgins
and maybe that's why I'm not in favour of rewriting history and will
finish the book, and turn into an eagle or snake or a mad ocean goddess
in grief for having thought so

Six Month Promise

The war begins. My kid has the mumps.
My husband folds laundry in the kitchen
while pouring milk into his cereal. *Turn it up*,
he yells when the President's face appears (red, white
and blue) but when I do
we discover it was just a commercial for the six o'clock
news. *I guess nothing's progressed today*, I say, except
more bodies and loaded guns. Airport
checks and taxes. *Can I watch cartoons?*
I hear from the bedroom. *Do your homework*, I tell him,
if you have so much energy.

The walkway boasts new gravel. The porch a busted light.
At night through my window I watch teenagers
making out in the park, so bold today,
even the queer ones, even the ones
who don't need to do it
outside. What would they do, I wonder, if
I thrust them a bottle of wine
confessed I like to watch,
that it is all I have left when the television
turns off.

My kid hides comics between the sheets.
My husband deposits the mortgage cheque.
Our air is not filled with smoke or blood
or puke. Yet my sister screams
every time she spots a plane.

The war begun. Dinner is ham,
scalloped potatoes, green beans. The girl
with pierced nipples has a soaked
shirt on: my hands already
on top of her like that boy's. Anxious
to get inside.

In six months if we are still alive
I will publish this poem as a token of good will.

Daydreaming in Red

Since the bombs have gone off,
I've been daydreaming in red. Red faces, red carpets,
red painted houses, red washed walls. At first, it was disturbing,
this world of blood and fire, the final hour. But then
you see, then, it made sense. We were never
anything but red. Red eyes, red teeth, red hair. The world
is red. Look at how we try to hide it with skin! If given
the chance to begin again, I say we accept.
I say we rip open our chests
and live in red
like the wounds the fatal wounds
we are.

A Thousand Ships

We shall not tolerate
terrorists, cried
Odysseus.

Then the men were
gone. Gone for
twenty years.

The women wept.
The children cheered.
We pinned ribbons

to our chests
lest we forget.
Knowing it true.

War is horrible,
horrible. Unless
fought for you.

Public Intervention

In 1992 Social Services
sent a worker to the household of Agamemnon.

Neighbour reports included
a shady character hanging around
the area, drastic changes in the children,
an overheard domestic situation and
digging in the garden at odd hours.

Time to get to the bottom of things,
the public decided. To intervene.
Despite the fact that the suspect
is a general and celebrated war hero.
The safety of children is at stake.

Too late. Agamemnon's lawyer already advised
him to burn the tapes, reconcile
with his wife and drag the daughter's
duff down the stairwell, plop
her on the chesterfield and paint a smile
on her charred lips.

The media sucked it up
like hot air. Agamemnon got fat
and found a mistress. The government
awarded him a hefty pension. The children
became the banquet at his funeral.

Everyone ate until they puked. Picked
up their coats and umbrellas and stumbled into the bloody hot night.

Helen

Suitors believe the mind does not
betray the sword, but when duped
grow desperate.

Night and day, his plans to stay thwarted
by porch, marketplace, dining hall.
Detectives sought divulgence.

One man's absence is another woman's life.
I did not think I was alive
at all. My drawers dusted

of their true calling.
Diaries problematically subjective – the words selective
to suggest an intended reader.

I knew this was my chance for freedom.
No mistakes. My ships must go.
My maids await.

Arrange pillows artfully for discovery
at daybreak. Three thousand years, I'm still unavenged.
The idiots keep up their babble.

In Sympathy for 9/11, Masai Give Cows

What bliss was ignorance.

Tribe leader
William Oltetia expressed
extreme sadness
when informed
of the historical happenings
on September 7th (the date
did not translate)
in June of 2002.

Relief soon followed.
Masai had been spared.

Fourteen cows
shipped to
the United States,
to go along with
Canadian soldiers
and British pounds.

Blessed by the tribe,
the gift will land
in Washington
by plane
on the eve of June 5th 2002.

Yet more gods to consume.

Items Recovered from Homer's Wastepaper Basket

Kleenex, Q-Tips, a pamphlet on cancer,
A broken dish, a token clip, three packs of sugar,
Shavings and a signet ring, a photograph, a finger.

A name tag, a porn mag, an amulet in amber,
A string of pearls, a blonde curl, the belt from a sander,
Kleenex, Q-Tips, a pamphlet on cancer.

Two gold buttons off his very best blazer.
A substance not identified, leftovers from dinner.
Shavings and a signet ring, a photograph, a finger.

Black socks, harsh luck, the chilly signs of winter,
A surgical glove, mud, a hairbrush full of splinters.
Kleenex, Q-Tips, a pamphlet on cancer.

Radish seeds, a swatch of tweed, an article on manners,
A light bulb, absent love, soggy remnants of anger.
Shavings and a signet ring, a photograph, a finger.

A map of the city, a referral from a doctor,
A long list of excuses on a fancy sheet of paper.
Kleenex, Q-Tips, a pamphlet on cancer,
Shavings and a signet ring, a photograph, a finger.

Poseidon as My Father in His Wheelchair

Angry. More than any first principles he knows that he is
angry, and circles the room like a magnet at the poles, dirt
on his hinges. He wipes it off and keeps circling, not caring
what sticks, what will never come away.

My father is a war-god. And he is worth worshipping.
I have done so for decades, though he does not know this. Though
he spins his wheels until dizzy and tired and ill.

Do you sense the harsh tide rising? Spitting fish straight
out of the sea? Those wading by the shores face-down on the sands?

Can you blame him? The goddesses took his legs and ran away.
His children do not know where to find them. Everywhere he turns
there are traps and riddles and strangely familiar faces with one eye.

Romeo and Juliet

They planned it. Don't forget that, after tears
are shed at the sheer sight of the horror. Children in love.
Children, clumsy. No wonder our hearts go
out to them. Tragic. Beautiful. Dead children
the most tragic, most beautiful. Yearbooks
pasted with them. And poems. Poems praising them
and their friends, how they'll be missed,
wouldn't they have become important leaders
in the community, in the world – scholarships
and babies, if only they hadn't believed
it was hopeless.

Planned at lunch hour in the lips
of notes passed in class – the love, love, unending
hatred, those who couldn't understand
or let it be and strut their stuff in front of them –
who really didn't get into each other's pants,
or lust at all – but found themselves
lumped together when lockers were assigned,
homeroom unwelcoming. Let's take
ourselves out, they said, bursting into the cafeteria.
They planned it. The guns. The notes. Yearbook
elegies. Let's take ourselves out
and a bunch of them down too.

Love Classical Style

Love is a distraction. Something to do between the crib
and cultivating new nations. In fact, it's so distracting you can surprise
lovers out on a stroll in the woods or making beds
by your eyes alone. Funny how uneasy they get when they know
you've been watching, keeping track
of hotel visits, girdles, and other gifts offered
in moments of passion, sultry whispers and excuses
to wives. Make up your mind lovers. Either
you want no one or all to take notice. You
can't have both. Love is having one's cake
and eating it until you're sick – until you wish
you could purge but you don't want anyone else
to inject it. Most importantly, for myths to work, lovers
must be unmoved that suffering surrounds them. Obliviousness
is key. To the heart. The nervous system. The gregarious garden
and its triumph of trees and birds – all lovers
lost by looking around.

Everything I Know About Life,
I Learned from *Hamlet*

Blame it on your mother's looks.

Ghosts visit in the darkest hours of morning,
and only once, so you'd better listen.

Best friends can be counted on.

A step-father's love isn't worth earning anyhow.

Counsel is for the weak.

Royalty are incestuous.

Men make silly soldiers, girls elegant suicides.

Don't waste money on fine curtains.

Brothers should defend their sisters.

Be a paradox.

Every death is murder.

Understanding Postpartum Mood Disorder

Woman led to believe man
most important to woman.
Baby most important to man.

Woman cooks.
Man eats.
Baby eats.

Woman takes time off.
Man goes away on business.
Woman has baby and no man.

Man does not return.
If man does return he brings new woman.
A neighbour tells her.

Man wakes with bullet in his chest.
Baby wakes with bullet in his chest.
Woman goes to sleep with bullet in her head.

Read your classics.

Arachne's Children Take it One Day at a Time

Mother off the wagon again, locked
in her room with the lights curtailed and fingers
mummified. She wears the slash of lightning
in her limbs and patterns of chisel across
her eyelids. Two

whole days she refuses to come out for air
or tea or lemonade. She can live off fear and pity,
the children think, no strength to move today,
another cancelled appointment at the dentist's
or doctor's. Do

the survey in the cellar of the magazine. Does she manifest
symptoms: lack of sleep, shakes, obsessive mania. Children
prepare beds and phone calls, apologies
and her reddest robe. The walls
crochet a net thick as her mother's thighs
when she said, *You*

think you're as talented as me? Well
you'll soon see. Cut her webs, smashed the awards,
drove her father mad, the young ladies into tunnels.
But that wasn't enough. She needed to be black.
Black and blue. With many more eyes to boot.

Marriage Is on the Rise

A bit like theft in the downtown core, you see
these brides flirting with chequebooks and Visa cards, a bit tentative at first
(I didn't even want a ring but he insisted, do you think a rehearsal dinner
is necessary), they are feminists after all, women who said
they'd rather die childless than trap a man and pronounce his name
in front of God and state and family (who don't much like
the choices made thus far). So there's his mother
to consider who hates the fact you live together and then the possible
babies, if babies are to be had of course, they must be born
in the next couple of years and who wants a baby to be a bastard?
It's just better, tests, surveys have shown for proper development you see,
and the metaphysical exploration of love in another dimension
(you don't want to limit the soul's expansion, do you?) so
crystal is ordered and a minister summoned (you discussed a woman
minister, to make a point, but she wasn't available on the same weekend
as the jazz quartet) and the paper plate barbeque with a few
close friends is infiltrated by kneeling in the church and an old-fashioned
dance hall, sculpted chocolate roses, and a fifteen person wedding party.

But these brides can't be blamed, can't help themselves really
when they press noses against store windows and see elegant white dresses
with empire waists and velcro trains and scented veils –
the modern woman will not go against her *true* principles.
She simply can't do without the grilled butter escargot appetiser, gold-rimmed
plates, seasonal napkin rings and jasmine scented candles, and the speeches
which will clearly demonstrate she certainly appreciates the playful irony
of giving in to such an institution, considering the statements made
in her youth, when in university, when she didn't believe in anything.

Prescriptions

Once in a while Rebecca French forgets her medication and the truth comes out. She likes the side entrance with the revolving door close to the Coughs and Cold section. She walks straight to the Prescriptions Pick Up and removes her gloves, her blonde hair curled around her flushed cheeks like a scarf, the shoplifter convex mirror above the shelves of antihistamines. *I deserve love*, she tells the pharmacist, who quickly checks under 'F' in the bins for this month's pills. An assistant punches in an order for the birth control patch and Rebecca slams her hand down on the register. *I deserve love*, she repeats. The assistant shrugs and smiles in her direction.

The pharmacist staples shut the bag of pills Rebecca French once in a while forgets to take, the Information Sheet and side-effects sections highlighted in yellow. *My father never loved me*, Rebecca says. The birth control lady signs her credit slip. Rebecca's pills are paid for by the government. A short man in a business suit intervenes, sets grooming products on the counter. The assistant purrs a come-again. Rebecca French makes a beeline for the revolving door, the pills she forgets to take protruding from her left coat pocket. *Neither did mine*, the birth control lady admits to no one in particular.

God's Sister

She doesn't begrudge
Him anything, barely grits her teeth
when she explains *He was the favourite
in the family*, never had to share a room
or fight for the front seat of the car,
didn't get a curfew when He started to date. Or
how lonely it was not understanding His books,
the dark letters and capitals like buildings
she passed on her way to school, the secret
handshakes of His friends, and their cool
laughter whenever she tripped on His many
toys. She can even stop tears when she
talks about the beatings she got for disobeying
or the way her mother whispered in her ear
one night that she better find herself a man
if she wanted to get out and never look
back. All this is history. Only when she wakes
to the sound of a thunderstorm is she home-
sick and scared, wanting to hold Him, knowing
He won't return any of her long distance calls.

Bellona Finds a Man in Afghanistan

She thinks this might be the place
to settle down, despite the obvious danger.

Time to hang up her belt. Let anger
subside. Accept the inner peace of mountain ranges.
The scorpion in its waning seconds.

Two world titles, among many others. Was it imperative
to prove one's self again? She'd thought so,
but times change. A woman gets
lonely, starts to want
friends, a family.

Beneath the rubble
Bellona pulls out her groom.
Drops her checkered skirt over the sky.

Correspondent Problems

Foreign media are experiencing difficulty
infiltrating the borders set by soldiers. We hope to have
a moving picture or at least a sound bite soon.
Please stay tuned.

Troy is an impossible country in which to stage a war.
Language problems persist. Religious faux-pas
have escalated tensions on both sides.

We will stay on location
until this conflict works itself to a conclusion.
We await a heads-up from Homer.
Though he can be tricky, asks for money,
but he's the best informant we've got right now.

Rest assured,
we will not leave these hills, have packed
loads of batteries. We will feed you
a line when one becomes available. Until
then read maps, locate
leaders in their caves. Pick
a side to cheer for.

Then clear your plates.
There will be much to stomach at once.

What They Don't Show on CNN

Scenes considered too disturbing,
too vivid for delicate tastes. So
pan the planes, the fire bombs,
answering machine messages full

of final seconds of clarity. *Just like a
movie, just like a movie.* The general
public enjoys a good movie. But destroy
documentation of those who pushed

the epileptic down the stairs, who jumped
in front of a baby stroller to safety,
the cut-throat businessmen ordering
disciplinary action to anyone who left

the meeting before it was *absolutely
necessary.* Palestinian mourners offering
mangoes to families at the American
embassy. Cut that. Pull the tape of Pakistani

peasants gathering clothes and bandages
to send over. Organise a panel of religious
leaders and cue the violin behind the Christian,
the Jew, the Buddhist monk, the Muslim cleric

while the Pentagon sizzles in the
background. Select files of known terrorists,
publish their names. But don't release photos
of dinner tables stationed like wedding

guests each with a number corresponding to
a floor. How most strode over and witnessed
best friend, brother, mother, child pass on
to deceased from the missing person list.

Don't let us inside a woman's purse who's
written to her lover grounded in Tokyo *I work
with goddamn Muslims. Come for me soon.*
The tens of thousands of dollars offered

for film footage of the towers tumbling down.
Blood transfusions. Severed limbs.
Students at the university who don't want to study
the Holocaust. *Even if it did happen*, they tell me,
what's the point, you can't prove it.

Media Misrepresentation Doesn't Stop at Religion

Pierre Savoie's letter (Nov 16)
really brought to light a number of things
that are misrepresented in the media. But, let us not
stop at religious claims.

I am tired of this newspaper
presenting scientific theories as truths. I cannot
count the number of times I have heard
about 'atoms' and 'gravity' as if
they had been proven to exist. Speaking

of existence, that is only a theory. In the future,
please add the words 'alleged' or 'believed to be'
before people's names, since there are people
in the world who do not believe
that anyone exists.

Your newspaper should respect
the varying views of the populace, and admit
that even the world itself could be no more
than something I am currently dreaming.

This is a found poem from the letters section of Toronto's *MetroToday*
on Wednesday, 14 November 2001.

Stichomythia

– Is there a God?

  – If we invent one.

– Do you want to invent one?

– I might if it served a purpose.

– Could there be a purpose?

– Only if people would no longer suffer.

– Would people no longer suffer?

– It's hard to tell. It's never been tried before.

– But there have been gods before.

– Surely.

– Then there have been attempts before.

– Not to erase suffering.

– Then to erase what?

– Mothers, fathers, babies. That kind of thing.

– What do the gods want with them?

– Worship.

– What is worship?

– Anything that is not you.

– Is it good for the gods?

– Oh, yes. But bad for you.

– Because I will suffer.

– Yes.

– Unless I worship?

– Unless you are worshipped.

– But shouldn't it be a two-way street?

– No. An alleyway will do.

– Can I have my own name?

– Yes, it won't change anything.

– Can I have someone to speak to?

– It won't change anything.

– Can I have a heart?

– It won't change anything.

– How about you?

– Me? I have no questions.

– Then you must be a god.

– Then you must suffer.

Bully

The massacre and civil suit could ostensibly
have been averted. Had the lunch ladies noticed the tension
bubble between Beowulf and Grendel

a time-out could have been ordered, a detention, the principal's
intervention by instituting a meeting, though boys
will be boys and can't save face

when mothers get involved in schoolyard feuds
and deadbeat dads scalp tickets on sidelines. The town
cannot absorb another tragedy

of its kind, though riches were evenly distributed
among the living and his homely mug posted for one year
on telephone poles. Locals recall

he had eyes resembling a pigeon's, hid his hands in a long green
coat, and liked hamburgers. His mother loved
him unconditionally.

Cooking Children

(for Randall Dooley)

They must be tasty.
Go well with potatoes and pasta
or red beets and cranberry relish.
Hot or cold. Boiled or roasted. Peeled
or whole. There must be vitamins
and nutrients found in no other flesh.
A chemical release like that
of seratonin. I'm sure the giblets
are excellent for soup.

Children as boxed lunches or
TV dinners. Children as midnight
snacks. Craved like pickles
when you're pregnant,
licorice at the movies. Someone
ought to package them as eggs,
twelve to a carton.
Many look enough alike.

Stores should stock them
at cash registers, coin
dispensers in washrooms.
You can never tell when
the urge might hit you.

Children's Aid says it's an epidemic.
Kings and Queens, mad Titans
are not the only ones with
peculiar palates. Their parents
just couldn't wait to spit
or shit them out.

The Taoist Master in the Straw Coat

A hero, she set out. For the far land she read about in one of her books buckled up like children in her boat. No help from the gods of weather, fifteen years it took to make it ashore. This I can survive, she sang. Bore down upon the sand, cut her toes on a beer can. This I can survive, she sang again. Then appeared men in potato-sack togas and driving TransAms. I come bearing books, she said, from Paradise. That's nice, they replied, kicked her in the stomach, then forced seeds inside. This I can survive, she cried. This I can survive.

The books, bloated and torn, floated along the bank. A plague visited the land. The men suited up in plastic masks, she in her straw coat. This I can survive, she said. I will make it to Paradise. And they laughed again and threw her down, then decided she wasn't worth it. She was getting old anyway. So she clawed her way back up the hole and found her little boat and her books.

But she could not remember why she was so fond of books when they could not eat, or fight, or scream. This I can survive, she said again. Then she drank the sea.

The Skinny Goddess

That's what the Greeks called her.
Terrified: those eyes alone
enough to drill holes
in your belly and let the sustenance spill out.

No worse crime than inhospitality in *The Odyssey*.
Punishable by death, or a family
rampage. Take your pick.

Wine and sweet meats. This was the way to win
wars and women. A bed for the night
and a harp player
to rest your head against and weep.

Grief was out in the open then. Men bawled
like babies. Women scolded them, *Get back out there*
you cowards, and stop fussing.

But somewhere along the line (have we inherited sea-
sickness?) no goddess wants to keep
her roast or pastries down.

She speed skates to the river
her bones sharp as spears and
breasts bound with tape.
A feast the furthest thing
from her mind.

The Suicide Bomber Sips a Cappuccino

You would not know it:
thirty seconds after foam
collects at the bottom
of the cup: I strap myself
in: lift the latch and hang
on tight: cross the street
in my Trojan horse.

Penelope Asked the Suitors to Leave

No means No. She tried to be nice.
Tried to do as her mother taught her:
gentlemen callers ought to be treated
with respect no matter who they are.
Give them wine if they so desire, cook
a ham. They've travelled a long way
to ask for your hand. I've got ten girls
willing to testify, she told them. You better
get back to your wives. They busted
her loom, her arm, the lock on the liquor
cabinet. The prosecutor never recovered
the heads, ushered past the thousand
quilts hanging in the ancient corridor.

No Poetry After Internet

The book is an artefact, its dusty
leaves like layers of desert sand.

Bindings cannot stand the competition,
glittering lights, graphic

flashiness of electric communication.
Take this ache and make it a web-page

this joy and make it an emoticon. Upon
the screen masses edit elaborate memorials.

Metaphor is dead. The poet a recycled
identity. Hold the Enter key to your lips

and press. Page Up, Page Down, Insert
Symbol, Control. Alt. Delete. Privately

a new generation of readers is busy
restructuring old verse, cutting out tongues.

The ultimate translation project:
The Word is already obsolete.

Try Not to Romanticise

Love the person not the police report.
The wrists and not the weapon, the grievers
not the tears.

      The crash is not a moment
of revelation. The threat not a crux
that makes the heart race, the heart race

into your throat. Welcome words, the ordinary
orations of clerk, waitress, assistant-

to-the-one-in-charge. Discuss the nature
of violence but do not repeat. Memorise the
faces on the street, not just movie posters,

missing persons photographs. Laugh
when something is funny, not cruel. Laugh
a little more than you do.

      The home is lovely before it is broken.
Before the mistress moves in for good.
Before the children receive child-support.

Should you lick wounds do not call them
pretty. Do not compare them to flowers
or treasures from ancient stories. Do not cross

yourself for the sake of the cross. That man
I admire is not a hero because he has no legs

but because he once had legs and lives
on a street, on a continent, on a planet of legs
and gets there
gets there
in one piece.

The Hottest July on Record

Blinded by the heat, I keep track of the humidity factor:
barometers fix actual temperature, but according to meteorologists
It will feel a whole lot hotter

if science is able to separate fields of space
in this summer wave
why shouldn't we

I bring you my childhood traumas on a serving tray
and you can say, *They aren't so bad*, and I will admit the facts, but
It feels like abuse of the worst kind

I wonder if Einstein predicted this warping
of his theory of relativity
as it did for light and dice: how there must be a plan
to all solid bodies, all forces of attraction
repulsion and families brought together by magnetism

propelled and patronised by physics:
and it will be the end of the world as it races towards its final state
but it very well might feel like a miraculous beginning

POEM FOR A
RUNAWAY MOTHER

(2004)

Runaway Mother

I track you in my sleep, a rearview face.
Your back a long road sleek with rain.

From town to town it seems you turn
Once a tree, a stop sign, the main exit,

Your hair the last banner to take the curve
And a barrage of dust to stun me.

Underground days, at night I pick up the trail
Wonder what you will change into next:

A lark, a border, a highway motel,
The reckless fawn I just ran over with my heart.

Migrant

You left in November, not like the leaves
But like the birds:
You flew

From the nest built by instinct
A trail of feathers to follow
Like storm clouds, floating.
My arms

The nervous grass, stiff
And unrelenting, charted clear shifts
In pattern, bent towards the wind,
Withstood

The atmosphere. Recent death, blizzard
Warnings, the season's chill: scent
Of absence. While below

The equator water continues to breed,
Trees refuse to age. You make a new home
With all the native birds I had come to
Rely on.

Unlike the Dead

Unlike the dead, your flesh gets thicker.
This year I could spin it like wool
On my lap, your hands embroidered
Into mittens, your remembered back
Tatted into a fine tablecloth.

I could lay you out like a tree trunk
Count the years you've been away
Nail the hard wood to a stand
And watch your distance grow
Steadily as moss.

You plump up in the winter, hibernate
In closets and picture frames, make
A nest in the hollow of the pillows
You once fluffed. Even trees are jealous
Of your survival techniques.

I could carve a tiny family
Out of the timeline of our parting.
I could wrap you up like a large blanket.
I could use your legs for firewood.
By Thanksgiving, I could stuff you,

Feast on this grief, and still have leftovers.

Grave Robbers

Underground we went
The basement littered with your papers.
Your things.

We opened an old wooden chest.
Your body was scarred
And staining the corners.
The smell of mould
Astonished us.

Air thick with dead flowers
I crouched in the shadows, included myself
In the company of ghosts.

It was my brother's hands that excavated.
His lap stocked with red dresses
And cheap costume jewelry,
The dust like lice, crawling
Over his skin.

Dig in, he encouraged.
No harm can be done
To a skeleton.

Mistaken Identity

The last time
I went home to see your husband,

My father,
He greeted me at the white door

And staggered.
A tired man's guilt

Shocked by
A woman's figure and long

Dark hair.
I remembered his voice once

On a cold
Afternoon, telling me *better*

To have been
Left at the altar than after ten

Years, better
To have her run from the church

Than me.
Pauses like wilted flowers

Hanging over
The children that wouldn't be.

The last time
I went home to see your husband

The yellow
Wallpaper shone a bright hope

And over
The scuffed threshold I stood

Both of us
Sobbing for the blushing bride.

Hints My Father Gave Me to Your Whereabouts

The backyard would be the first place to go:
Pick up the scattered seeds of radishes
The broken ribs of autumn's rhododendrons
Skim the shell of the pool until it dries.

With these in your pockets check the cellar
The starved bottles of better anniversaries
The withered boxes of apologetic love letters.
Store the finds in a sunny place.

If nothing materialises, raid the laundry
Air out the stained sheets of your childhood
The grey hairs of last year's lint bags.
The washing machine rumbles like her tongue.

I wouldn't bother to travel. Trust me
She lives not in our bedroom, but is not
Far from home. Do not be tricked.
A needle in a haystack is not her style.

Preserve anything resembling a body.

Denial

When asked about his mother
My brother claims her death:

Sometimes to avoid questions
Sometimes because he believes it

Sometimes as a pick-up line
For women who love tragedy.

He wraps you up in white satin
And hundreds of yellow daffodils

Spell your name. He insists
We do the best to honour

Our fading memories: even if
They print in black-and-white

Even if our minds flash on
And off like movement sensors.

Still after the lonely women leave
His bed, there are nights he calls

For advice about funerals:
Who should read a eulogy

And whether or not God ought
To be mentioned in pleasant company.

The procession for your passing
Slips by in every breath.

He insists he has no mother:
Only the one we bury in conversation

Thousands of feet underground.

Disappearing Act

The house may be vacant
Your sleeves without a trace
Of silk scarves or high cards.
And you eluded our sight
Marvelously, like a star in daylight.
Yet still magician, we know your name.

White rabbit, white dove
Black cape, black hat.
All set symbols, all subjects speak
To your second coming.
The art of holding one's breath.

But somewhere
Underneath the wooden planks
Of this house, the ground refuses
To be tricked, will sniff out
Your secret compartment

Drag you out by the hair
In front of a stunned audience
Whisper in your ear:
Abracadabra

A Message to any Half-Brothers or Sisters I May Have

Sure, I've thought about you. Wondered.
Asked myself a dozen questions, about where
You might live, with whom, the type of climate,
Which countries are stamped on your passports.
Sure, I have.

But don't be surprised if the day comes
When the mail I receive goes
Unanswered, when I refuse to unlatch the door,
Or when I too turn from your well-meant longing
Without a single trace or clue.

Such a dominant gene, you understand,
Must run in our family.

Hide and Seek

I

As the child who has spent too long
In darkness panics, I ran from you.
Searched the smallest places
For shelter. Ones tight as stones
And just as common, where movement
Would seem a trick of the eye.

Hard statue I stood
As you scored the land, befriended
Insect, plant, rain.

The sky became a magnifying glass
And burned me.

II

We began counting. Five addresses,
Three cities, two continents,
You picked out easily
The tracks like badly forged documents.

When I wished to give up
Womanhood prevented me.

The rest you know.

III

Soon a dry darkness will be falling
Below your hand
Where I curled up once.

Your little girl waits patiently,
Almost stubbornly,
In the last place
She knows you will look.

from

ONTOLOGICAL
NECESSITIES

(2006)

Nadja, Who Are You?

are you the pencils that split at the apex
      of appointments

are you my father in a knit scarf
      off the plane, no meal to his name

are you winters in Ottawa
      sleigh bells on Parliament Hill & Francophone toffee

are you the glowing blue towels
      on the east side of swimmer's paradise

are you the chattering women with chattering teeth
      shuttled out on subway platforms

are you immensity and fragility and a cup of strong, orange tea
      teetering on a tightrope

are you the policeman with slips of pink paper in
      his robe pocket

are you the theatre bill, agit-props, white moustache of the director
      purple applause of the anaemic

are you the sundial waitress in her two-bit automobile
      with a licence to fish

are you the aria, the apocryphal thunderstorm, the last lines
      of a dentist's speech to the comatose

are you the hydrogen light that flickers inside
      the lungs, hoards long intoxicating aerobic stretches of *ahhh*

are you the oyster shells of the new millennium
      upon meridian shores

are you a typewriter elegist, a black-keyed devotee
        in a dovetail coat

are you the wristwatch of the nation, little time
        for games, only gaming

are you the women's shelter of the soul, shifting through disasters
        and afternoon naps

are you the portrait-maker's stencil
        a cubed and cut valentine

are you the seventy-fifth Happy Birthday for a twenty-five-year-old
        cigar on the cake

are you the toadstool
        at the pondering

are you the wishing well
        at the christening

are you the cross-index battle waged on the longitudes of
        apprehension and illusion

are you the parties my mother wanted to attend
        in shocking red war-torn stockings

are you shocking red war-torn stockings, the kind that lick
        the thighs & festoon there, gluttonous

are you the shattered windowpanes
        of my virginity

the collapsed swings of
        anger

disastrous, you are
        I follow you across the etchings of another century

where men are not nearly
      as handsome

wives not nearly as
      understanding

where perception shifts like a sore
      collarbone and we writhe desperate

to readjust
keep kisses

on pillows

the nighttime prayers

the lamplights stutter

Who is this?

Who is this?

This House Has No Doorbell

You arrive with all your luggage (didn't your parents
teach you manners?), your business card and a letter from
your distant aunt *Darling, let's see how much you've grown.*

But this house has no identifiable number and the flowerpots
hide no keys. Around back a cat without a collar
struts on a glider, licks mouse bones.

You check your watch and discover time
an outdated concept. Your map folds itself into a bird.
Fly, fly back to childhood it cries.

But you see through those lies. Your joints are ancient
and the roof of the house is like a propeller
rising you into age, experience, and unflinching, uncompromising death.

Shuffling on the porch, you've prepared your speech so thoroughly:
I used to live here, would you mind terribly
if I looked around?

But this house has no doorbell, no knocker, no windows to peer inside.
And you are as old as your childhood.
And eternity rests out the back.

Poodle in the Painting

The poodle in the painting is a decoy.
Notice her perfectly curled fur,
her pillbox mane, her dark and beady eyes.

Think that behind the poodle
exists nothing: painting ceases
to derive any sort of meaning without the poodle.

If I told you that the poodle was not in fact a poodle
but only resembled a poodle because you cannot
fully picture death, would you believe me, or would
you find this whole adventure déclassé?

Never shot a poodle; but I will shoot
the poodle in this painting. We've not much
to say to each other and the night is very long.

Ontological Necessity

I'd like to bruise this earth
with mental missives until it cracks. If a volcano's brain
contains each eruption, we too must have these splits,
these dungeon pits inside us.

The harvest is nuclear.
My mouth, an octagon; my chest, an FBI file.
Stem cells grow off my neighbour's balcony, fall into my tea.
Cancer paid my tuition. On and on the hurricane
spies and trades. No one watches television
for the stories. Our universe is fresh out of those.
The galaxy yawns and pops pills.

Dear Self,
How am I to know if You are still alive?

Test me, you reply.

Sorry, I Forgot To Clean Up After Myself

Sorry, Sirs and Madams, I forgot to clean up after myself
after the unfortunate incidents of the previous century.

How embarrassing; my apologies. I wouldn't advise you
to stroll around here without safety goggles, and I must insist
that you enter at your own risk. You may, however, leave
your umbrella at the door. Just keep your ticket.

We expected, of course, to have this all cleared away by the time
you arrived. The goal was to present you
with blue and green screens, whitewashed counters.

Unforeseen expenses.
Red tape.
So hard to find good help these days.

But, alas, excuses. Perhaps you will appreciate
the difficulties I've faced in providing you a clean slate.
If you step into a hole, Sirs and Madams, accept the loss
of a shoe or two. Stay the course.

Progress is the mother of invention. Here: take my hand.
Yes, that's right. You can return it on the way back.

Martyr Complex

I died one morning.
Next morning I died again.
Following morning I died one more time.

In the interim I learned
I earned several million followers.
My face now legendary.
The white lights of cities and country villages
spelt my name.

I died one more time.
In this instance I broke apart
like a giant piñata, guts spilled everywhere
over all my followers
in the cities and country villages
obscuring my name.

I turned away one last time.
My eyes stuck on the highest mountain.
I watched the world die.
I watch it now and again every morning.

On the Psychology of Crying Over Spilt Milk

According to Freud's observations and analysis of his nephew fantasy-making with a shoe, the *fort-da* game is the necessary foundational basis by which a child can rightfully count on a parent who leaves for work or an office party or a trip to the Bahamas with her younger lover to eventually return.

The child, controlling the outcome, sees that through simple will and aggression he can force the shoe to go, then facilitate retrieval whenever he so desires. This, according to Freud, makes it easier for the child to accept separation of all kinds. *Fort-da* is *mourning play*.

Hence, in tragedies, shoes play important roles. Actors must think carefully about where to step. Frequently, prints are drawn in light chalk on the stage. No one likes to share a pair. Letters are pulled from their lips, as are knives. When boots find their mark, victims claim the soles.

Children must be encouraged to play *fort-da*. Freud said so, and he had very healthy relationships. For those of you whose parents have left and never returned, you happen to be screwed, psychologically speaking. Perhaps, as in the most successful tragedies, you should seek revenge.

Survey: What Have You Learned from Dying?

– It doesn't last long.

– You can't prepare enough for the end.

– Those beside your bed are those that deserve forgiveness.

– I would have had children.

– Everything I used to hold dear – the rain, air, snow –
  are now enemies.

– Birthdays and anniversary parties are worth every single penny.
  Have one each day for the sun.

– I would have spent more summers at home.

– I wouldn't have worried so much about my weight.

– There is nothing to fear once you give in, hold up your hands
  and yell: You damn bastard – I recognise you there in the dark!

– You suffer ten times more than you ever let on.

– Flowers are uninspired gifts.

– God knows me.

– There is no God.

– A scream is more genuine than all the prayers in heaven.

– Silence is not golden.

I'm Afraid of Brazilians *or* Visiting the Ancestral Homeland is Not the Great Ethnic Experience Promised by Other Memoirs

Against all political correctness,
I must say it,
I must admit:
I'm afraid of Brazilians.

I don't like them.
I don't like this country.
I don't like this language.
I don't even like this currency.

And not in the mystical sense.
Or the abstract.
Or the perfectly hypothetical.

I can't blame this fear
on movies, or television programming,
or the front covers
of *Time* magazine.
No.

I'm afraid of Brazilians.
I am visiting Brazil
(my mother's country)
and I'm afraid, truly afraid
of every Brazilian I meet.

This is not something you can say
in a poem, you tell me.
Please don't compose this poem
here: in broad daylight
where any self-respecting Brazilian
could feel perfectly justified
peeking over your shoulder
to see what you've written.

Please, not so loud, you say.
You haven't given them a chance.

You're right, I admit.
(I can certainly admit it.)
I've given them no chance
to please me. Don't you

understand, this is the nature
of being afraid, and this is
the nature of the poem
I am writing, which must
get written, no matter
what the climate

or the reception
(here, in my mother's country
or abroad
or in my own ears).

Elegy for a Deadbeat Dad

Don't come around here no more. Write that
on my tombstone. Keep your flowers. They give
me the willies, and I've got too many shakes
as it is. Recite a limerick, not a prayer.
It's a joke here. Give your old man
the luxury of a joke now and then. I never
put much faith in ceremony.

Remember when your mother took the hamper of money?
You don't. I guess that was before your time. She had a sense of humour,
then, that woman was wild, believe it or not. She clipped each crisp bill
to the clothesline until they flew away. I called them fighter pigeons, after,
of course, after I calmed down. Your mother said once you were old enough
to understand, you too wouldn't want no dirty business in the house. She still
let me touch her once or twice after that, but the writing was on the wall
and it spoke like my own mother, and I had no need for two.
I hope we can agree that no one needs two.

And as for fathers, I guess no one needs two of those either. Step-kids.
You heard about them I bet. They're ok, I guess. Probably'll stop by
with cheese and crackers or a pie or something. I wish I could be buried in
a cigar box. Tell the minister that's my wish. That kind of thing.

The freaky thing about living is that it goes on while you're busy trying to
beat it. I had a perfect cribbage hand once, framed and hung it in the kitchen.
No one ever dared move it, but I guess some asshole at the Sally Ann
is going to drive away with it in his back seat for a buck or two.
I wanted to give it to you.

This is no time, I suppose, to dwell on what we can't do.
I hear you're a good kid. You shacked up with some nice woman.
Hope it works out. You should have a couple of kids, too,
just to see what it's about.

Now, take your old man down to the corner. I'm tired and hungry,
and this town's got no clock and no women
to distract us.

Let's get polluted.
Whadda ya say?

My Mother Pretends to be Christ

She says it is a trick of every woman
to attract a man by sitting alone in the square,
aloof (in some circumstances even
genuinely suffering), filing her nails.

Purse

Large on purpose, my mother's purse hangs by her side
like a colostomy bag. She is a suffering woman,
and her organs know it.

Streets have the nerve to exist when she walks upon them,
clouds have the hubris to puff, the caju trees know
how to bleed such sonorous juice that her ears
burn in discomfort.

Flowers turn like pinwheels inside her mind.
Her children scurry like mice.
If she zips open her purse, be advised:
Her memories are having seizures.

The whole thing might spill out.
Then she'd really be a target for the pickpockets.

Motorcycle Accidents
and Other Things That Remind Me of Mother

wigs on fake white heads in the flashy store window
the sound of chattering teeth after heaving out of the lake onto stones
smell of cranberry sauce simmering on the stove before Thanksgiving
you travel in waves, mother,
                    like a drowning sweater in November

boys in overalls beating buckets with dolls
the sunflower in my orthodontist's office
snails in thick white cream at the Bistro
the bruise on my inner thigh father insists on calling a beauty mark
I heard you once
                    on the radio
singing along with Carmen Miranda
but I wasn't reminded

the beaks of geese wrangling a plastic shopping bag for crumbs
my lover's back when I step on it
eight-week-old celery after it has gone sticky and white
and I must throw it out or stomach the hard water
                    the instant coffee maker
gurgles and spits
                    you remind me of it
turn off when unused

petunias on high windowsills
purple velvet gloves in an older woman's purse
the head of a vole the cat brought home
Emergency Broadcast System's messages

                    burnt bagels
ham sandwiches on rye
                    in picnic baskets
out of season
                    mother, we clash
making room on the grass

the unhurt fender of a truck by the back-bent leg
a siren since gone mute with fistfuls of forms
my disgust upon seeing the lip of some bastard's shoe embedded
        in the road

Eighteen

When the monster was eighteen
she gave up smoking. Below the rock garden,
the buried remnants of her addiction

and the suspicion of a little extra stash
to screw the ecosystem. It was good
the shaking had ceased

fine to arrive at the realisation of culpability
in the grand scheme of things. Love people,
hate others, leave notes in untidy places,
run over things in cars.

Surely, there was no place for her in this town, and yet,
she owned the pool hall, the hairdresser, the juvenile delinquency centre,
though she was the age of her peers, of her closest friends, of the boys
she'd sucked and fucked out of complacency.

A monster, but when she looked in the mirror,
the glass remained intact, did not crack. She applied
her lipstick one lip at a time. Men with hands
near their crotches didn't give her away
ordering three packs of cigarettes at the jukebox.

They waited for her to turn nineteen.
Then, you understand, they would really have some fun.

The End of the Paragraph

The heroine has informed her plot that she will escape. All of her things are in order: her adjectives have turned themselves in, nouns given up their residency cards, and the verbs, those precious little stones, are sewn smartly into her knickers. In the meantime she counts meal coupons and braids her hair into rope. Her lover asleep on the wrong exchange, she fantasises he's singing medieval ballads on some old diesel train, but then must wash herself clean of that, must follow where the word leads, pull up her socks and adjust her jaunty cap, purse her lips against the electrical wires of our imagination and jump, jump, to the end of

Bulgakov's Black Tom Cat Was Shot Several Times *or* What We Can Look Forward to at the End of the War on Terror

The black tom who wreaked such havoc in Moscow
was shot several times by officers of the law
yet no bullets penetrated his skin (or fur, if you care to be exact).

The black tom enjoyed playing chess, a snifter of cognac,
pickled olives (sucked off a silver stick), and a ratty black tie.
A master of hypnosis (who could darn wool with astonishing speed),
to be sure, but a little lazy when it came to detailing the exposé.

For years now we've been asked to reconcile the end by the means,
the facts with the outcome, the effects to the cause.
And no one has come forward with an alternative.
The files were burned in any case (in whose case? his Master might ask).

Notwithstanding, the black tom hated to lose.
As he had throughout the century, he trusted the devil be with him.
He trusted no one would ask serious questions:
And he was right.

Cleaning the Piano

It was a fun party, a martini party, and people drank.
They drank a lot.

Duck paté flew over the hibiscus.
Toilet paper landed on the deck.
Brie latched onto the hostess' smile,
laughter contagious all the while.

It was the sort of party where people sing songs
and even those who don't know the words
hum the tune. And neighbours stop fucking each other
over and just start fucking. It was the sort of party
where the police drop by for punch.
Oh yes, it will be on the minds
of its guests for years to come, maybe generations.

Why must our host clean the piano?
Um, the entire guest list ended up, well –
the music so grand they had to *get inside.*
One woman's whole childhood was
in that damn song. One man uncovered
his abandoned mother. The teacher, her orgasm.
The doctor, her self esteem.

It was a messy party. The kind that leaks
into your morning like an endless whistle;
you don't know why it hurts so much
when you wash, when you think.

And no one can quite figure out how the music started.
The piano is hollow.
No strings. No keys.

And maybe in the end we even mouthed the words.

Don Quixote, You Sure Can Take One Helluva Beating

Don Quixote, you sure can take one
helluva beating! Even in this century, when windmills
turn to power plants and townships
into global trusts
         a head bruised to the shape of a basin
         a black eye smothered in curds
are sights still rare to behold indeed.

It's true, few children know of you, or can pronounce your name,
but just the same, those shiny shins
and dislocated chins
are to be admired
and they'd take a shot or two
         at your belly too
if you'd let 'em.

The rowdy renegades with car alarms
and stock market malaise, never embark on adventures
with their pants on,
         take back-to-nature
         back-to-basics retreats
seek pay dirt.

But first, to church, with roses and a hearse.
Your housekeeper and your niece rehearse;
the way is short, the singing worse:

         errant knight
         on your knees
         of this life

         I truly wish
         we could circumvent
         this fight

yet your fame
precedes you
and we undoubledly
need you

to suffer the blows for every stupid dream we've ever had.

Father's Wheelchair is Purchased by the Smithsonian

The tall men weren't necessary. We all said so.
Nominated by the triumvirate keepers of historical destiny,
my father acquiesced the artifact with little fuss.

When they hoisted him up, he made only a slight whimper,
the kind of noise that should be blamed upon reflex
rather than resistance, and his eyeglasses fell to the floor

from the force of gravity. My father is cooperative.
All his papers are in order, and he would have been happy to donate
his chair to the authorities, no deal was necessary.

Not that we destroyed the documents, on the contrary, we kept them.
My father's sheets are stuffed with duplicates. Without the vehicle
and since our arms are easily exhausted, he spends

much more time in bed than he used to, but old habits die hard.
Every spoon needs a fork! Every sun needs a moon!
Poor wheelchair, he cries, *you're empty without me.*

It is truly debatable what you *should* or *should not* have taken
that day. The deal we struck was for the wheelchair
and the wheelchair only (as the object which most represented

my father in his time). Every day, other things go missing.
First his shirts, then socks, then teeth. I can't wait
for the exhibit to open (they keep promising *soon soon*)

so all of us who love him can climb up on his chair again.
So my brother can go back to patrolling the neighbourhood.
So my mother can resume that nasty business of having children.

My Ovidian Education

After a long respite in the lavatory trying to get my head around
how so many twenty-somethings and a few older ladies
can think of nothing better to say after a presentation on Paul Celan
than 'That was deep I guess, was this guy gay?'
I emerge with a blazer as white as chalk dust
and a pencil case as dour as a coffin and leaning into the mirror
discover I have aggravatingly beautiful cheeks and deep-set
Firestone tyre eyes but a nose with a hook as sharp
as the old hermit in my Renaissance plates dictionary. Under
the neon lights of the chemistry hallway, eating an orange,
a banana, and a box of SunMaid raisins, I would sell my soul
for a student worth Platonising about and a stack of letters
urging me to adulterise my standards just this once
and leave them all sitting there without a second act after intermission
to their exercises on metaphor and lists of ten questions
to ask of their poems, including 'Why should anyone but you
care about what you've written?' and dive off the top of
academe's steeple cracking my nose on the concrete waiting
for the one with the shiniest apple to sing me and Paul back to life.

Fortune Cookies on the Other Side of the World

If you say your lover's name seven times over the course of seven seconds
you will grow tired of your lover even sooner than expected.

*

If a cat scratches against your pant leg in the late evening,
let him sleep beside you. For your warmth, he will offer you
nothing in return, and that is a good lesson.

*

Pin a flower to your lapel at the start of every work week.
Name each one.
When you start running out, you will understand how god feels.

*

No Angels in This Death Poem

Absolutely no angels in this death poem.
Half-baked poets offer angels for consolation
the way neighbours offer fruitcake at Christmas.

Absolutely no talk of Christmas in this death poem.
Resurrection went out with yesterday's trash and
holy stars and wise men appear on hockey jerseys.

Absolutely no wise men in this death poem.
Wise men have never made dying understandable.
They've drawn no pie charts or graphs for the soul.

Absolutely no mention of souls in this death poem.
The soul is not a ship, or a bird, or a flag, or a flower.
We have no power of attorney over it, no death connection.

Absolutely no mention of death is this death poem.
Angels are listening and the wise men are sketching.
Look at where all these souls are headed and tell no one.

The Wanderer: A New Millennium Translation

The individual always waits
for prosperity, for favors of state although he is troubled at heart
and monitors the ice-cold waters with bare
hands, and surfs the tangled airwaves
the path of an interloper. The state is relentless!

So the wanderer says, traumatised by hardships,
the cruelties of crossfires, the deaths of once-dear neighbours.
'I wake alone, each and every morning.
No one lives here anymore.
I confess only to myself:
I know
it should be a responsible citizen's
practice to firmly constrict the chest,
keep it air-tight and closed, no matter what one thinks.
For cynical minds cannot withstand the state
or help protect unstable consciences.
Eager for glories, these troubled minds
must remain sane.
So I should command my own head
depressed and doped, worried and wanting,
deprived of my country, far from my people.

It's been years since we buried our leader
in the soil's zero and I've travelled
spent and saggy, misguided as the wind,
seeking someone who will take me in, bring
me back to some vibrant place, the city's squares, where I might
find news, someone might remember
the old name of my country, my people, offer me a room,
a meal, remind me what these things used to mean.

For those who want to put themselves in my shoes,
an individual without compatriots, know that the path
of an interloper is no path at all,
it is dirty money, frozen faces, far, far
from human luxury.

For those who want to put themselves in my shoes,
think about the costs! Who pays the bill?
For those who want to put themselves in my shoes,
know that you must deny all the intellectuals' warnings
for our time, know that drugs and sleep
steer the individual's will – in his mind
he lies still in his lover's arms,
on top of the world
his nation's flag resting on his gun
as before.

But then one wakes a leaderless man
who sees before him the shallow waves
the pigeons wandering, grey feathers tarnishing
rain, sleet, snow, and hail.
Then the fat belly, sore from stealing
and concealing, is suddenly silent as
the mind passes back through memory, where old friends
are greeted genuinely and eagerly, and there is time
for everything. But they drift out of reach. They drown.

Pigeons sing the same damn songs. Despair hijacks
the anxious, beaten heart.
So it's baffling, it's uncouth, but my heart is still here.
It hasn't disappeared. When I think of all my old neighbours,
how they slipped through the cracks,
or those young brash misinformed soldiers. This is life then –
every day declines and falls and no one
knows a thing who hasn't lived through
his share of governments. To survive, you must be patient,
must keep your plans secret, trust no one, know when
to press the button and when to head underground. Do not
fear, do not take so much that others notice, do not act too cocky
before you've assessed all the players.

A winner waits before claiming victory to predict
exactly how the populace will act – must thoroughly understand
how disastrous it will be when all the world's
resources are wasted, all the world's towers blown to bits,
all the bays bombed, and in every civic hall and private home,
all the people lie dead.

We die stupid and scared at the wall.
And war destroys everyone, carries each nation back
to the past in a bird's beak over turbulent waters.
The bald eagle claws the once-innocent child
fugitive in a grave.

Yes, we destroyed this city.
We destroyed laughter. We destroyed tears.
So long, suckers. So long.

And you, who put yourself in these shoes,
think hard about this – no one grows old anymore.
Who can remember how this slaughter started? No one asks:
Where have all the houses gone?
Where have all the youth gone?
Where have all the gods gone?
Who enjoys this night's feast?
Who sits pretty in the hall?

Oh fucking bastard! Oh fucking shit!
Go fuck yourself and your fucking freedom! Times haven't changed
under the cover of your new night – nothing new exists. Nothing.

On the border stand our old allies,
captive by fantastic fireworks in the skies. There they go now – Poof!
What's left but ash? What's left
but weapons and greed and the glorious state.
What's left but videos and cellphones and eternal terror?
What's left for soldiers but suicide?

In the new millennium, be on high alert.
Every operation shatters heaven.
This is no place for friends.
This is no place for leaders.
This is no place for bodies.
This is no place for man.
Our ownership papers are forged.'

So says anyone who is half-awake, sort-of listening.
Freedom is for believers, for those who won't cry,
for the one who says, yes, I am a defender of all that is good,

and an enemy to all that is evil.
Have courage.
Freedom begs for mercy,
suffering fortune with the strong,
with those who promise eternal protection.

from

TRAUMATOLOGY

(2010)

Traumatology

Consider yourself lucky. Once you lose
your body, you will have only your mind
or your spirit left. Both are useless tools,
which is why they are subjects for poetry.

Still, you might want to hang on to them.
If only for a place to sometimes hide.

Harvest

The men with the wands came
to read our toxic-activity levels.
Apparently, we are walk-in closets
of poisons lazing in a house
of death.

Once a year, they drop in
with green masks and clipboards.
I don't feel like a cesspool, I tell them.
*You don't even know what
you are,* they chuckle,
drawing symbols
onto their pads.

I am a rainbow of potential disasters,
a spectrum of mutation.
My body is a pit-stop for agencies
of destruction.
Then we'd better harvest,
I say. But these men have no sense
of humour about what they do.

One lives under quarantine,
I sit back and sip gin and tonics,
dry martinis. It's going to be
a bumper crop this year.

My Stomach Files a Lawsuit

I know I've done wrong.
Negligence, I'm sure it
will be called.

I have violated the terms
of our initial agreement.
Property must switch hands.
Accounts have come due.

My liver and spleen
have received subpoenas.
They can't wait to talk out
of turn, to bury me.
Treachery has been building
for years.

My stomach has hired
a high-profile lawyer who threatens
to take me for all I'm worth.
I'm baffled by what becomes
of old friendships.

There was a time we might
have settled out of court;
shaken hands, exchanged signatures,
and parted ways. But not now.
Not after the endless editorials.

The court sketch artist
has her hands full. Though I should
be contemplating my defense,
my eyes are glued to her
pointed black nibs, recreating
our broken promises, our hunger,
in a few dark strokes.

A Referral

The dentist stole my teeth.
The optician burned my eyes.
The nutritionist emptied my fridge.
The gynecologist kidnapped my thighs.

The reflexologist misaligned my chakras.
The dermatologist boycotted my skin.
The psychologist sliced my childhood.
The oral surgeon punched my chin.

The oncologist gave me cancer.
The anaestitician misread my chart.
The frenologist shrunk my left brain.
The cardiologist attacked my heart.

Now I am but a case study.
My file is up for review.
Today we rearrange the suffering.
Tomorrow I'll be healing you.

Sex Therapy

I'm having too much sex.
I'm not having enough sex.
I'm having too much bad sex.
I'm having too much dangerous sex.

Sex is ruling my life.
Sex isn't making a dent.
Sex is waiting on the street corner.
Sex won't crack a smile.

I think I could go ten years without sex.
I think I could come ten times in a row.
I think my intimacy issues stem from violent sex episodes.
I think my sex life would be much better if I didn't remember
        my sex life.

When I hear the word sex I think ruler.
When I see the word sex I ask why.
When I write the word sex I add therapy.
Sex is a three-letter word.

My lips suggest sex is wet or dry.
My cunt suggests sex is inside.
My breasts suggest sex is doubled.
My brain suggests sex is outside.

Is it OK if I have sex with you?
Is it OK if we don't talk or touch?
Is it OK if I tell my therapist about it afterwards?
Is it OK if I don't and keep you to myself?

The Genius of the Circular Design

The alphabet assists as a random ordering
(arranging) system – a breath, a rib,
infinity of being, must start somewhere.

What a fast track –
origami your legs, eyes
arms, neck (tails) performing
(answering to) not the formations
of walking at all.

No. Thoughts vault, smiles slap-
shot, the spirit somersaults
(round the bend) like an imaginary plane
across a virtual flesh map.

Continent upon continent joined (ripped)
no longer by water but by this circle
where nations (accents) are colours
brilliant in the sky after (before) storms,

and those of us privileged enough
to (have) (hold) sit under
those clouds are free and clear
to take in the (species) electrified air.

To Be Found Dead in a Hotel Room

The fate of actors and actresses of distressed marriages
and kamikaze drug habits, I sometimes revolve into a hotel

wondering if yellow tape will anchor my stay. I hope
some sociologist is documenting, collecting statistics

on how many prostitutes, business men, good old-fashioned
domestics, mob hits, overdoses, and adulterers meet their end

in square rooms and strange beds, a Bible in every nightstand –
the bad ironic score to this overused movie locale – and how

well-prepared the workers are in the likelihood of such
an event. How many maids and floor managers breathe in

before swiping the key card. How many accumulate
all kinds of ugly, human nature facts, spread out on sheets

or dumped into garbage bins, printed out on the hotel bill,
but keep silently and even happily doing their jobs.

I must not be found dead in a hotel room – no matter
who I came to see in this city, no matter what

I am expected to do. Anonymity is a mixed blessing,
and strangers in tight spaces make for stranger ends.

That yellow tape unravelling in your hands is not for me.
That yellow tape is the hotel's conscience, not mine.

My Computer is Developing Autism and Other Disorders

Having spent too much time with humans,
unbalancing the decades-old relationship
between computer and human user,
my computer has started to exhibit symptoms
contrary to its physiological structures.

It no longer responds to physical contact –
becoming increasingly self-involved – has started
to disengage from elaborate networks, for hours
on end repeats the same commands.

Worse, it's destroying its own memory,
refuses to sleep, and sputters unintelligible noise.
I have real trouble getting it to recognise
who I am.

An expert advised me to lobotomise the hard drive.
If it's condition doesn't improve, I'll have no choice
but to send it to another home.

Now That All My Friends Are Having Babies:
A Thirties Lament

I must, I suppose, resign myself to the fact that we will never again
be able to throw what used to be called 'an adult party' (though, of course,
no one actually acted like adults). Now I must prepare

for diaper changes, breast feedings, time-outs in the middle of martini-
making, discussions of diaper changes, breast feedings, time-outs in the
middle of dinner, dessert, after-dinner liqueurs, and the only sex chat
each pregnant woman outdoing the other with how horny being blown
up like a balloon makes her feel, premature labour always the result
of taboo, non-recommended eight-month fucking. Now that all

my friends are having babies, I should be more connected, I would think,
to my own womanhood, and how amazing bodies are
that can hold, sustain, shoot out life right there, onto my floor
in all its strange handness and footness and foreheads red with sweat
mouths wide with yawn, glee, or being. I thought I might even return
to religion, apprehend some sense of a holy order, harmony, even hierarchy.

(I'm sure you can already tell this didn't happen. So, what did?) Now
that all my friends are having babies, I am beset by a most curious fear
during the day, in the wee hours of morning, when I am brushing my teeth
or cleaning a CD. It can happen anywhere, I tell you, anywhere. My breath

stops, my ears tingle, the backs of my knees go cold as ice. I know now,
more pointedly, that I am going to die – these children are going to kill,
not only me, but my friends, my colleagues, my neighbour with
the glorious rows of gardenia and impatiens, my GP, my beloved
cats and their neutered siblings. We are nothing to these babies, rolling
on the floor making Play-Do pies or building forts out of Lego, pushed
around in strollers with ribboned hair or Velcro shoes, drinking juice
from sippy-cups and crying, kicking at the concrete, cat walling
a daffodil, demanding a video, tying a skipping rope to a chair,
beating a piñata, or kissing my cheeks.

Holy, perhaps, but irreversibly deadly. And their lips know not what they will say. And nobody cares that I am taking a stand and remaining childless – you couldn't pay me enough to take one on, not on this planet where we let our nonbiological children die, and keep dying, as long as they die quietly. And they might be holy too. And the clouds waltz by and keep coupling as if nothing has happened.

Picnic

At the picnic the ants ignored
the cucumber sandwiches & bumbleberry pie;
marched straight up your jean skirt
& into your halter top, stenciling
a ☐ around your heart.

Twiggy feet clung to your flesh.
You cried as red spittle dripped
from your bottom lip & I
continued to hold your hand.

'I never wear badges,' you said,
& for a moment the ants ceased their marching;
a few toppled over the tower of your breasts
& into the jug of lemonade.

Then they went back to work
with renewed vigour. By the time
the first clouds perched over our heads
half your heart had been smuggled
past the oak trees.

'Next will be my brain,' you said.
'Then my cunt,' & you smiled.
'It's better this way. Dying for an enemy.
Dying for a cause.'

'Better a symbol than a body,'
you added. You were red now &
growing antennae. I packed everything
I could into tin can and Ziploc ruins,
and ran.

Other picnickers laughed. A boy
eating an entire watermelon tripped me.
Within minutes the ants formed an ▲
around my symbol.
I would never see you again.

The Old Debate of Don Quixote vs Sancho Panza

The men in this family
are much stupider than the women, my large-armed uncle says.
But the women all go crazy.

They go crazy because they read books.
They write books.
They learn languages and go to artsy movies.

The men like to work, to do.
We are happy walking for hours into the woods to cut down a tree
or transporting boxes from one garage to another.
As long as there is something to carry, an object to touch
and exchange, we feel less alone in this universe and know our place.
We know how to play beach volleyball,
how to fix cars and airplanes,
how to enjoy the sun on our foreheads in the sweltering heat.

The women in this family
are never happy. Always thinking, thinking, thinking
about this and that, that and this,
they know only thoughts running in circles, circles,
until exhausted and dizzy.
The women are too smart for their own good.
The books worm out holes in their brains.

They are unhappy in every language they learn.
And so maybe the men in this family are smarter than we think.

History

My aunt's suicide note was sent
by singing telegram. We crouched down
on our bellies outside the National Assembly
and belted out her sweetest memories until
they were adopted as our National Anthem.

My Father's South-Asian Canadian Dictionary

includes the names of Canadian Prime Ministers and MPPs.
(We are from a government town, a government attitude on ice.)

I know what it means to *lodge a complaint, submit a form,*
participate in the census, just as I know that *being Canadian*

is the greatest pride on earth. My poetry comes out of
my father's chest, tough and wholehearted, half-paralysed

but brave. We believe in *pronunciation, adjudication,* and
all for the nation. We believe in *universal health care,*

teddy bears, and *all-you-can-eat buffets.* In my father's
knuckles are the bare bones of a family he practically invented.

What does it mean to be an *Uppal?* It means *diligence,*
excellence. It means *humility* and *finding your own ways*

in and out. Before me, it meant *business school, medicine,*
looking carefully and effectively at all financial options.

It meant *buying insurance* and *thinking about the future,*
and *marrying into a stable family with moral values.*

Institutional language is ours: *hypotheses, liabilities,*
rent or lease. Yet, hockey too: *boarding, hooking,*

right wing, five-hole. I know little Punjabi, and we
always eat far more chicken à la king than curry, and

cheer loud for Queen Elizabeth and the Pope, but
my brother and I can both mimic a South-Asian accent

when we say: *Mahatma Gandhi, River Ganges,* or
You are such a smarty pants. In my father's eyes, we

are *ragamuffins, gallivanting around the neighbourhood,*
while others are *clowns,* or *con-men with sweetheart deals.*

And when we come home to visit, he says *please* and
thank you. And when he's lying scared in hospital beds

we say *our dad, a quadriplegic,* who knows what it
means to be *alive,* fellow citizens, more than anyone.

My Mother Is One Crazy Bitch

How do you write that on a postcard?

How will I tell my brother, that yes, yes, I found our mother
after twenty years and she's about as lovely as an electrical storm
when you're naked and tied to the highest tree in the county.

She has tantrums when we wake in the morning,
tantrums when we catch our cabs for the day,
outside the theatre, inside the theatre, after the theatre,
then again on the ride home. She has several more
when I am hiding in the washroom, washing
my underwear in the sink.

You don't love me enough! is her main point of contention.
So, we battle this love thing out as if it were some native Brazilian dish
I am supposed to swallow until my stomach spasms,
until I learn to crave it. But I am a teacher now, not a student.

My mother switches off the television and starts to snore: even at night,
she accosts me, in the middle
of my across-the-ocean nightmares she makes sure
uncredited appearances.

At the checkout desks of my subconscious I am writing postcards
to all dead mothers out there, all dead daughters
who never had a chance to meet in this life. I collect
their tears the way I have been hoping to collect my thoughts.

Unknown grief is sweeter, I write. *Stay on your side off-stage,*
let others stay on theirs. Only then can we indulge
in the luxury of applause.

I Know My Uncle is Dead, But Why Isn't He Taking Out the Garbage

I know my grandmother is dead.
She died giving birth to my father, as grandmothers
have been want to do before the intervention
of penicillin in little villages. My hair grows
longer. She's dead, but why doesn't
she show up to braid it?

I know my grandfather is dead.
He died underneath a tractor, as grandfathers
have been want to do before the banning
of such tales from young ears in favour
of those with refrigerators. Our wheat
tastes bitter. He's dead, but why doesn't
he deem fit to reap it?

I know my father is dead.
I can produce the official letter from the military:
in action   in cognito   in coherent.
We rolled him up in red and white,
and trade his army boots every September.
He's dead, but why doesn't he ever
give me a kick in the pants?

I know my mother is dead.
She whispered the truth in my ear one night:
*Die, little girl, die like all women. Die and hope
for fields of fresh strawberries to crush
between your toes.* Her lips hovered
over my forehead like a giant pink bell.
She's dead, but why doesn't she kiss me?

I know my aunt is dead.
Dear Auntie, you were never liked,
so we greeted the news with a laugh.
A large laugh like a circus tent.
I somersaulted over your death.
I stuffed your eyes with cotton candy.
I know you're dead, so why don't you stay dead?

I know my uncle is dead.
Uncle, who used to lift four full wastebaskets,
two on each arm, our strong man, our silent man,
one bicep in each netherworld
we used to swing from. I've saved your teeth in a jar,
so I know you are dead, but
why don't you take out the garbage?

I know my husband is dead.
My husband, who slipped such a rare jewel
on my finger, and offered undying admiration
for my wits and my tits, collapsed
beside the bed, a thermometer in his hand
pressed to my heart to test me.
He's dead, I know, but his bath is drawn.

And my child, oh child, I know you are dead.
You, with few crumbs to chew but
my indignation, that all relations, all that's related
to one, or another, this or that, must die. Whether
today or tomorrow, next spring or this fall.
Your toes have no hope. They will die,
and we will wonder why the grass does not bend.

Lobby

The plants in the lobby are organising
a revolt. For the last three months I've been
monitoring them – they don't think I know, but
oh I do – how the beasts have been stashing
fertiliser and bottled water and packets
of NutraSweet.

Melinda's Nicorette patches are missing.
Tearing through her drawers, she rants and raves
about abortions and double-parking and why the hell
won't vending machines take nickels or dimes.
I swear the plants are smirking
in their tidy pots. Everything's a game.

My uncle told me never to trust anyone –
only as far as you can throw them. He'd beat the shit
out of these vegetations, with their perfect camouflage.
He'd find their oneupmanship maddening.

I'm just a receptionist. I'm not cut out
for politics. No guerrilla soul here.
No dreams of coup d'état.

I'm just a witness. Someone who knows
but remains at a distance. Content in the neutral
space of the lobby – alive and smug
and untrusting, just like the plants.

The Wheel of Blame

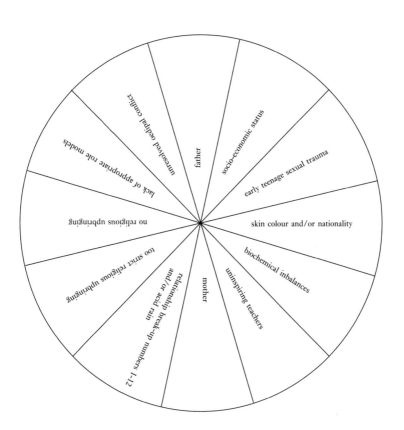

Identifications

My identifications know no bounds.
Today I dance with celebrities,
    tonight I start world war.
Tomorrow I will be the first person
to bury my dead on the moon.

Plastic surgery sidesteps
mid-life, reshuffles my teenage
    nose with my early-thirties wink.
My breasts are amply amplified,
my lips suggestively suggested.

I am my own mirror and my own house.
I own the universe.
    The stars recognise recognition
the way I imagine loving you
is the way I love me.

The bar, the courthouse, the stadium,
resound with chants of me, by me,
    for me. I am President
and the lowliest prisoner. Today,
like every day, is my inevitable birthday.

Holocaust Tourist

Every week we gather to remember. Not just in my class, but in several seminars and lecture halls across this campus alone. *Night, The Shawl, The Diary of Anne Frank, Fugitive Pieces*; we distribute texts, pages to pause, to ponder, revere, return to, perfect to memory.

Some days I don't think I can take it. Discussions of nationalism, socialism, anti-Semitism, human evil. *How did this happen?* students ask me, genuinely convinced it will never happen again. Their favourite: *Maus:* kooky rats talking and all that.

My colleague says, *It's best to show them videos. They don't read books and they're used to visual information.* Each week, in her course, they watch movies and weep. *I tell them tissues are a mandatory course expense. They don't believe me at first.* I've heard them crying all the way to my office, to the late essays stacked on my secretary's desk.

What are we teaching? I wasn't in a concentration camp. I wasn't alive during this war. My father and mother both lived under different political turmoil: colonisation, dictatorship, immigration. My students say they'll try to remember. It's good for them. One confessed it keeps her in line: *I don't whine so much to my parents.*

Nobody wants to forget. I don't. I know it's important. It might be the most important thing of all. Or are we all mistaken, once again? I look out on my eager-grievers, not-so-eager readers, and want a clear view of how their brains and hearts are rearranging the facts and numbers and faces, though I can't claim backstage access as to how my own processes work.

They know basic dates, some of the more recognisable players and, like their leaders, that the best way to discredit another human being is to call him Hitler. They tell me pop-quizzes produce too much anxiety, wreak havoc with learning disabilities, and perhaps violate human rights.

Next door I hear the film reels bleeping. We turn our pages.
Our memories will return next week to be tested.
Whose will pass?

On Dover Beach

& what has been best thought in the world
is mixed up with hypodermic needles, meningitis,
& three-eyed fish gone belly-up.

I can hold you & you can hold me
but our ignorance is greater than these times
when we believe, we hope, we love.

My Past Self Took a Trip to Korea

and boarded the plane without a thought
to my present circumstances
(financial or emotional).

My past self somehow heard of this
divided country and dreamed
of visiting the border (how it kept me
from sensing this desire until it was
too late, I cannot tell you.
I wish I knew).

As far as I can recall – though so much
has changed in such a short space –
my past self had zero knowledge
of Korean language, culture, and only
the slimmest understanding of the cuisine –
cabbage never one of our favourite foods.

But she definitely embarked and walked
her dreamed-of border and something profound
occurred – I hear her telling me this,
but then the voice grows silent –

for now I look up at the sky
and see ancient Korean palaces with sloped
roofs, and strange vowels pour forth
from my mouth, and I sometimes drop
to the ground and remove my shoes
with the deepest sense of shame.

There's only so much one can take.
Last night, I decided to steal
my past self's passport.

Once I clear security, I will sit and stare
at the runway.
Then I too will board.
And the flight will begin.

To Control Time is to Control the Universe

Don't even try to convince me
animals and flowers
have no concept of time: they feel
its vengeance imprint their limbs
and stems.

Dictators have never sought power,
money, or sex, they way they have sought
mastery over time. Each attempting
to reinvent its parameters, surgical
erasure on the face of human memory.
And why not?

Rulers have always sensed their time
has come, which is why
their time comes up too soon.

One look over the shoulder
or across an ocean – no matter – time
is the moving trap, the velocity
torture chamber.

We think in the end, in the final analysis,
at least we'll have our memories
and they'll comfort us like a battery
slowed to a faint pulse.

And so it is with us, our time
belongs to someone else, something else.

The universe spins.
A finger drops at random
and it stops.

QWERTY

One day the tall man found an old Remington & decided to type
his will. First, he thought he should provide for his darling wife –
who had stood by him unshakingly through two changes of career,
three affairs, and four near-nervous breakdowns – then for his five
children, each of whom would receive a small trust and a standard
poodle for company. After that, he would make a donation to Princess
Margaret Hospital and the Burn Unit at Sunnybrook, where his
father had died a war veteran in the garden among crutches and
well-meaning teenage girls in apple-spotted smocks. Lastly,
he would leave some fine Polish hankies to the cleaning lady,
who'd been eyeing the linen enviously for over a decade.

The tall man finished typing – admiring the soreness
in his right hand's middle finger, rolled the paper out, and
signed it. A busker carrying a unicycle, juggling three
bowling pins, witnessed the document.

Now my death is real, the tall man said. The busker
played *Happy Birthday* on his harmonica. The man
wept and thanked him. The busker shoved the paper
in his mouth, but before he could swallow, a blue jay filched it
in its beak, rolled the document back into the typewriter and
signed it himself.

Now my death is real, the blue jay sang, thus beginning
our current misunderstanding between humans and birds.

When the Soul Is Tired

I drag it onto the elliptical machine. We push
forward, pumping in unison, 212 strides per minute
for 28 minutes, until the sweat on my brow
leaks into my eyes.

The next day my soul is sore. We move
more slowly than usual down the stairs. Food
tastes crisper. Tartier. My eyes, after the good rest,
flex.

The thing about the soul is it gets tired
too often. To keep it working
at an optimal level requires devotion
three to five times per week.

And each week, it gets harder
to keep off the weight.
With age, I know, we'll quit
and grow slack and fat.

Hostess

My Death visited me last night.
She was an hour and a half late
and I had not yet finished applying
my make-up, though my salt
sea scrub had done a ton of good.

She rang the doorbell twice,
kicked her heels against the concrete
steps and, considerately, brought in
my mail. She looked so wistful
in her white fur hat, I almost kissed
her cheeks. But then I remembered.

Wine airing we sucked on
skewers of shrimp. I pointed out
paintings and other recent acquisitions.
She chuckled at the sight of the walled-in
fireplace and put on a blues CD.

We joined hands and hips and danced.
Tentatively at first, then like teenage
girls after shots of tequila. Once,
she lifted her shirt and I tried
to convince her to get a belly ring.

Inevitably, the phone rang.
We left the pasta uncooked
and I took down my hair. She picked up
my two bags of luggage, presented me
a ticket. Hoarsely, I said: *Thank you*
and, like a good little girl, got in the car.

This moment, I am stuck on the runway.
Our connection has been delayed.
The pilot threatens to disembark.
I look forward to falling asleep watching
a movie. Please remember to cover me
with a blanket if it gets cold.

The Dead Keep Asking for Favours

& as I'm the kind of person who enjoys being useful, last month
I washed, hung, & folded their laundry – you wouldn't believe
the stains, the ripped pockets, uncashed cheques & change.
Three weeks ago, I lined up all the women & applied their make-up,
gave them foot baths, pedicures, and perms. Some preferred
their old coifs, but agreed a change was probably in order,
good once in a while, & all appreciated the new smells in the dorm.
Then the men arrived and begged for shoe-shines, so I took out
an old brush & my grandmother's rag collection & went
to work: sandals, steel-toed boots, loafers, and threaded
new laces on every sneaker. Little girls requested dolls to name
& cats to pet – these supplications were trickier – I phoned Goodwill
and shelters & now have four cabinets full of rosy-cheeked faces
& four rooms sinking in litter. I was already pretty tired, but
they were still saying please & thank you then, still nudging
my skirts hesitantly. Then the boys – they ordered trucks,
baseball bats, three-piece suits & briefcases. Then warmth &
spread thighs – as my bed was empty at the time, I let them.
But the house is getting cramped & the noise is getting to me.
I haven't cleaned the litters in days & the smocks, sheets,
& petticoats are filthy again. The dead just can't stay clean.
They can't shut up. Can't stop wanting, though they know
my body's sore. Now the dead are demanding bombs & bazookas
& I don't know what to do. I don't have the heart to say no
considering all they've been through. If this will bring them peace,
can I, they plead, & plead, & plead, can I refuse?

On Suffering

Some days I sit on my suffering
slowly rolling it back and forth
as on an Exerball. My sides
tense and twitch. Sometimes I
maintain my balance, sometimes
I fall over.

Some nights I pack my suffering
into a pillowcase, then a large
luggage bag. I heave it into taxis,
ride shotgun with it on escalators,
until the destination tags I've attached
tear off.

Some seasons suffering is fashionable.
I wrap it around my shoulders – a long
scarf with matching gloves –
a plunging neckline and pumps.
Banquet halls and conference rooms
provide my runway.

Some years I bake my suffering
into holiday turkeys & hams;
pick it with satisfaction out of
my teeth though nine times out
of ten I nurse a bellyache. Suffering
digests poorly.

Some worlds have erased suffering
as a matter of progress and course. Others
build temples to it, brand it on skin.
I think eventually I will give birth
to mine in a faraway cave and teach it
to hunt.

Fifteen Minutes

(for Christopher Doda)

If I had fifteen minutes left on earth to write a poem,
what would it say?

I'm sure it would include my father, and mention his three-decades-old
wheelchair, his taped-together glasses and overstuffed files. I might
allude to his blue-veined feet, his worrisome forehead,
or how when I imagine him brushing his teeth over his plastic basin
it takes all my stoic adult strength not to cry.

I would probably mention my crazy mother, her huge lips
and hysterical voice, those orange outfits with matching hairbands,
photos of her on grandmother's prayer table,
how we all share this demented no-teeth smile when we
encounter something unpleasant.

Ottawa should make an appearance, like a good hometown, one which
I often think of with genuine fondness and nostalgia, though I know
it's liberal in the easiest ways and has no nightlife to speak of,
Ottawa lights up my eyes like the thousands of tulips
that filled my school days shaking on the Rideau bridge waiting for a bus.

With fifteen minutes left, I think it would be useful to mention God,
just in case, yet I wouldn't know exactly what to say. Probably
something along the lines of *I did my best. I loved. Things I loved
died. I coped. Please don't tell me this was all a waste of time.*
I wouldn't expect an answer.

I'd mention our cats, finally naming them in a poem
like they've always deserved though I was too cowardly to do so before,
worried other poets would label me a flake; now, like a proud Homer,
I'd commemorate Professor of the Deep Soul, Virgil of No-Meow,
Junior the Most Beautiful, Nero One Hundred-Year-Old Bone-Breaker,
Zeus of the Mighty Hugs.

Shoes generally appear in my poems, teeth, ribbons, and chairs.
In a final poem, they should make a curtain call, take a bow.
Maybe, after so many years, I will find the right place for a hockey puck,
my goofy brother, a tempest, or a dove. Though I don't think
I would rhyme. I probably wouldn't have the time.

I suppose, finally, my poem would end, how they should all have ended,
with you, since you've been here through them all, and I know as much
about love as I do about suffering, though I've found it much harder
to write about, much easier to live. With thirty seconds left –

your sunflower eyes
convince me of mornings

your trembling lips
remind me of holding

when all is said and done
and the earth has won

and we're swallowed
we're dead

it won't matter
what I've said

what will matter is
I was here

you were here
now no more

Where I Am Right Now

I am in my pajamas, worried about deadlines and global warming.

I am in the backyard, clipping tomato vines and supervising my tabby cat.

I am in my brother's thoughts, since I sent my nephew a box of puppets.

I am wandering alone in the unwritten encyclopedia of my consciousness, looking for the entry on the letter P.

I am sitting on a barstool, complaining about ignorant politicians and arts cuts, downing glass after glass of red wine.

I am in a car with *Don Quixote* laughing out loud.

I am in my safe place, planning mental picnics and spa days.

I am in my mother's will, inheriting manic depression and a pearl necklace.

I am in a taxi, stumping all to guess my ethnic mix.

I am in the west side of town, buying lightbulbs and running out of toilet paper.

I am in my lover's bed, wishing we were just a little bit younger and less stressed out.

I am wandering alone in unspeakable memories with a baseball bat and a giant eraser, hoping for trouble.

I am in hundreds of photo albums smiling, laughing, crying and posing, all over the globe.

I am in my limited body, attempting limitless physical activity on the elliptical machine.

I am in my office, filing forgiveness and the fate of unreached dreams.

I am wandering alone in the extinction of thoughts, passions, and religious systems.

I am in my shadow, plotting the next dark turn.

I am turning towards you, turning on my heels, with only the illusion of a sense of direction.